ON TARGET

Mastering the Four Pillars of Business Success

Practical, Proven, and Profitable Steps to Go from Where You Are to Where You Want to Be

Rick McCulloch

David Shiang

ISBN-13: 978-1532743351
ISBN-10: 1532743351

This book was printed in Canada

Published by Entrepreneur Solutions, Calgary, Alberta, Canada

August 2016

Dedication by Rick McCulloch

I would like to dedicate this book to my son, Michael and my daughter, Megan

Dedication by David Shiang

For Helen, Katie, and James

Praise for Rick McCulloch's "Timeless Commandments for Entrepreneurial Success"

"… I was impressed. Great stuff, nicely encapsulated and easy to read and digest. I will be using it when I train National Best advisors. I will go to your website and promote it thru my social media channels. Nicely done. "

~Randy McCord. Business Director, Founder   National Best Financial Network

5 out of 5 Star Reviews on Amazon

"At a recent business seminar, I got hold of this great book which deals with almost all aspects of business. It simplifies a lot of information in a compact form, which makes this book an easy read. The topics will definitely open your eyes and inspire you to take the right action to grow your business."

In today's rapidly evolving business world there is plenty of information to digest. Only by continuously putting attention on learning, which is an absolute must, success in business will be achieved. By reading this book and getting useful advice from the author, you will save valuable time and grow much faster.

Here are three things that I learned and that anyone would definitely benefit from to grow their business:
- there are many shortcuts to entrepreneurial success
- the right marriage between visibility and credibility will   do wonders
- there is a big difference between working 'on' your business and 'in' your business

With plenty of reference to other well-known business leaders and authors, the author points anyone and any business in the right direction to increase growth."

~Jan Hendrickx, C.E.O., Business Success

"This is a great read for anyone starting out as an entrepreneur or the seasoned veteran. It's loaded full of simple, practical and insightful advice that everyone can benefit from. His thought provoking Principles force you to ask yourself the tough questions in order for you to be efficient and do what you, as an individual, are good at and outsource the activities that may not be one of your strengths. Highly recommend this book."

- Dan Moore

Skyrocket Your Business

Go to the link below to claim your free copy of Rick McCulloch's

Timeless Commandments for Entrepreneurial Success

TCfES.SkyrocketYourProfit.com

Table Contents

Foreword

Kerry George, CEO of the Canadian Imperial Business Network www.cibnconnect.com

When I read Rick's first book, *Timeless Commandments for Entrepreneurial Success* and I was deeply impressed with it. So impressed, that I recommended it to several of the business owners who are part of our networking organization at the Canadian Imperial Business Network. Over the years, we have seen many authors, business coaches, and marketing experts come and go at the CIBN, and few have left such a lasting impact on our members. Rick's book was not loaded with pages of fluff; it was real and practical advice that was simply stated and easily applied. Many found it to be a great value to them and as a result, he has become a recognized speaker at our Mastermind events and a trusted voice of wisdom that our business owners have come to rely upon.

Rick McCulloch has become an expert in his field. He exudes knowledge and is a capable leader with a storehouse of wisdom. I read this new book On Target - Mastering The Four Pillars of Business Success with great anticipation and I was not disappointed.

Business owners have struggles. We see it every day with our members and thousands of connections. Economic stresses beyond their control batter them on the outside. Lack of planning and strategy coupled with poor management can chip away at them from within. 80% of businesses fail in the first five years and the statistics over ten years are even more formidable. Marketing is key to their survival, yet the subject of marketing is a vast and incomprehensible beast that they know they need to master, but it seems a daunting and unrealistic expectation at best. Most business owners get bogged down in the day to day challenges of running their business and seldom have time to get above the ground map for a 30,000-foot overhead perspective. As a result, marketing campaigns are not planned out, and results are seldom measured. They are desperately treading water in a pool of over-fished, dirty mud fighting to survive amongst the sharks of competition without a method to differentiate themselves and get out into a clean blue ocean water where schools of untainted fish wait to do business with them and pile into their nets.

This is a book for the masses of business owners who are looking for a way to create a unique selling proposition that will position them beyond the reach of their competitors. It is a tool for every professional who wants to stand out in the marketplace as an expert in their field. It is packed full of ideas for your marketing department, and it will inspire the lone entrepreneur to reach for the stars.

Rick and David have used the Hero's Journey as a compelling method to help you build a story for your business. It is a bold and creative idea that Hollywood has been using for years to capture our attention. George Lucas and Joseph Campbell made this procedure a legend in the Star Wars series which has become a mammoth success that men, women, and children have been drawn into for decades. This book will guide entrepreneurs in creating a powerful business story that can be used in their advertising efforts giving them great impact in their markets.

Years of experience have given the authors of this book many insights. As they have worked with business owners and seen the rise and fall of good and great companies they have shared many stories of successes and failures. They bring to you the most powerful seminar tips that they have ever seen as well as the most common disasters that they have experienced. You will recognize many of the movie scenes and begin to understand why marketing has inspired you to buy in the past. You will identify with the nostalgia of past brands and see why you are compelled to purchase in the present.

Creating a sense of urgency is every marketer's dilemma. How do we move people to action? Rick and Dave point to successful campaigns from a variety of industries to give us the wisdom to build a marketing plan for today that drives buyers to buy. They show you how to feature attractive ideas and use phenomenal headlines or subject lines to draw consumers to you. They draw you into delightful, imagery, and spectacular examples that have become classics, and they show you how to integrate these concepts with the content that you are creating today.

This is a book that will do as the title suggests and keep you on target as you apply the four pillars of business success!

Preface

Spike Humer, Spike Humer Enterprises, former COO and Chief Consultant, Jay Abraham and The Abraham Group

Business has changed.

Same game but with new opportunities, new challenges. New rules apply.

Entrepreneurs and business owners who understand the changing landscape have a chance to survive. Those who learn how to master their message and their market are poised to become and remain the preeminent player in their industry. Business owners and entrepreneurs who ignore the changes in the climate and environment are headed for destruction and extinction.

Seem overly dramatic or harsh? My apologies for the stark reality-check. My intention isn't to be a doomsayer or pessimist. My role is to be a pragmatic realist and introduce you to realities, new horizons, new hope, and new most importantly—new resources and methodologies to help you succeed.

Indeed, business has changed. Online and offline, consumers, customers, clients, and prospects have almost unlimited choices as to where they spend their money. Literally, hundreds of millions of people are connected online, and tens of millions of people use the internet daily to search, shop, and have supplied their needs, wants, and desire. The way people buy certainly has changed but just as importantly, the psychology of how, where, when, and why people spend their money has been transformed forever.

In a rapidly changing environment having a solid base to build from is even more critical than in stable environments.

But having the ability to be agile, flexible, fast, and responsive is just as vital, today, more than ever.

Our ability to adjust and adapt has to be predicated on information and knowledge. We have to understand our market—who they are, where they reside and where they gather information, and how and why they buy or don't buy. We need to know how to capture the attention, lead the imagination and earn the trust of our prospects, customers, and clients. We must understand the value proposition of our products or services so that we can earn the trust of our market. Ultimately, it's essential we understand the platforms and channels of information and communication available for making our message most understandable, appealing, and actionable, as in generating sales revenue and ideally repeat sales and referrals. These are the foundational pillars of success for any business.

On Target helps any and every entrepreneur not only erect the support necessary to ensure performance and profitability, but this book also serves as the business blueprint for sustainability, scalability, and durability in any economy, in any environment, in any industry. The book is the right message at the right time for every business owner or entrepreneur who wants to increase their performance, enhance their profitability, and to connect with and convert their prospects into buyers and their customers and clients into long-lasting transactional relationships.

Introduction

Bill Gates of Microsoft once said that business is very simple. It consists of only three components: Revenue, Cost, and Profit. Take Revenue, subtract Cost, and whatever is left over is the last component, Profit.

Revenue - Cost = Profit

The goal of most businesses is to maximize profit or something closely related to it such as stakeholder value or earnings. Of course, it's easier to generate lots of profit when you have a quasi-monopoly, but our point it that business really isn't all that complicated. A lot of the advice you come across in books, magazines, seminars, you name it makes business much more complex than it really is. (The old saying "publish or perish" is definitely at work here. All you have to do is go into a bookstore or look online to see the massive number of business books that more or less cover the same ground. Fads of the day abound.)

On Target: Mastering the Four Pillars of Business Success is in some ways a continuation of Rick's highly-acclaimed **Timeless Commandments for Entrepreneurial Success.** However, it stands on its own. Like the earlier book, it emphasizes that business is about people, first and foremost. But rather than focus on the mental and mindset challenges that inevitably face all of us at some point or another, we focus on the psychology of the market, or to be more precise, the psychology of your prospect. We also provide specific timeless, yet tactical elements that you can apply right away as you grow your business. This book is about implementation, and it provides specific tools to help you define, describe, and run your business so that you can gain more traction and ultimately more profit.

Business involves an exchange of some sort, one person giving something to another in exchange for receiving something else. This has been true since the dawn of humankind. The details and mechanics of the transaction may vary, but it all boils down to wants, needs, and desires. Economists call it supply and demand. The scenery may change over time, but these are the fundamentals that you must master.

In this book, we're going to look at business as a human endeavor. We're going to start with principles that have been with us from the beginning and see how they underlie today's way of doing business. We're not going to get hung up in the latest technologies, fads, gimmicks, and passing fancies. Some of these are valuable today and may even be around in a few years, but many others won't be. Quite frankly, much of what marketers are trying to sell you are tactics and tricks that have no relation to strategy. You've no doubt seen advertisements as if they were written by a robot. The mechanics may be there, but the glue that holds everything together is missing. You may know what an autoresponder is, but if you don't know how a sequence of emails is meant to work on the minds of your prospects over time, you'll be sending out disjointed messages that are going to be ignored. You may have spent a lot of time and effort on crafting the finest emails only to find that no one is listening. In our view, far too much marketing is like that. We want you to learn the fundamentals so that your tactics have a solid foundation.

We're not going to cover the latest Facebook or Google hack that could go out of fashion in a week, a month, or a year. We're not going to talk about nurturing your prospects with a series of letters or sending gifts to your best prospects. Knowing how to do this is certainly worthwhile, but you can learn about them somewhere else.

Here we will combine business with psychology. One question we are going to focus on is "why do people do what they do?" If you can figure that out, if you can put yourself in the other person's shoes and see the world from their perspective, you are more than halfway there. We'll also include discussions about products, services, strategy, marketing, advertising, pricing, discounts, and offers, but we want to make this book as applicable to a broad range of people as possible.

Whether you are a consultant selling your services by the hour or the manufacturer of winter boots, a business can be boiled down to a very simple formula. Take a look at the following:

$$Revenue = Price \times Volume$$

Although the above is very short, it is deceptively simple. We urge you to think about it often as your business grows in size and complexity. When you determine what to offer your buyer from a dizzying array of possibilities, keep in mind that Revenue is comprised of two components that you need to keep a close eye on.

You will recognize the term Revenue from our discussion of Bill Gates above. Revenue is also called Sales, or Kaching. Henry Ford once said that nothing happens in business until someone sells something, and he was talking about the fundamental act of exchanging one thing for another. One of these things is usually money. In the movie Jerry Maguire, Cuba Gooding Jr. made "show me the money" a household phrase. Everyone knows what it means, even if the person doesn't know what a business is.

At its most basic, Revenue has two – and only two – elements. Price, the amount someone pays, and Volume, how many they bought. A business that sells 100 widgets at $10 each will have $1,000 in Revenue. A consultant that sells 5 days of advice at $1,000 per day will have $5,000 in Revenue. Pretty simple, right?

World-renowned marketing consultant Jay Abraham teaches that there are only three ways to grow a business:

1. Increase Price

2. Increase Volume

3. Increase Frequency of Purchase

We think that the last of these is actually a subset of the second. In other words, getting someone to buy twice as often is essentially the same as doubling volume. Since two is a lot simpler to grasp than three, we suggest that there are really only two ways to grow a business – increase Price and increase Volume.

Now there are an infinite number of ways to do this, and many businesses have their own unique characteristics, but if you don't distil Revenue into the simple relationship between Price and Volume, you are likely to get mired in a sea of complexity and confusion. No matter what you offer, you need to be thinking of how much you charge, how many people buy, and how often they do so.

Price and Volume are two main variables at your disposal when you think about bringing in Revenue, or as some might say, making Sales. If you think of yourself as a manipulator of Price and Volume as they relate to what you have to offer, you will be on the right track. Yes, Quality, Service, Margins, Value, and many other factors play their roles, but for the purposes of making the cash register go Kaching, Price and Volume are the important levers.

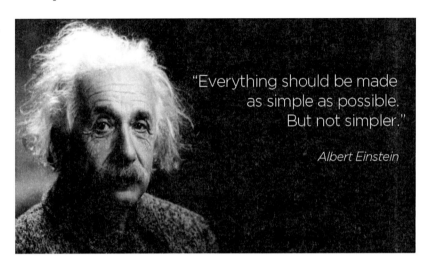

"Everything should be made as simple as possible. But not simpler."

Albert Einstein

Note: the above quote is often attributed to Einstein, but there is some doubt as to whether he actually said it. In a book of Einstein quotes, there is a section that contains quotes *incorrectly attributed to Einstein* and another containing quotes *probably incorrectly attributed to Einstein*.

In **On Target: Mastering the Four Pillars of Business Success,** we simplify business success by focusing on four key areas. If you can master these pillars individually and as a whole, and then apply them to the many nuances that are unique to your business, you are virtually bound to be successful. It doesn't matter whether you offer a product or a service or a combination of both. It doesn't matter whether you are low-priced or premium-priced. Now the devil is in the details, but you need to get all four of these pillars working in harmony together in order to have any chance of making it.

Ralph Waldo Emerson said, "build a better mousetrap and the world will beat a path to your door." You've probably heard this many times. This sounds great in theory, but there are two flaws with such a "my product will sell itself" view of business. Your Market needs to hear about your mousetrap (Merchandise) before it can beat a path to your door. And they need to have a mouse problem. If you can't get the Market's attention or if they don't have the problem you solve, no amount of Price and Volume manipulation will have any effect. It would be like selling air conditioners when the temperature is freezing outside. Or offering raincoats in the middle of the blazing desert sun.

Many companies, especially those in the technology arena, build better mousetraps only to find out that no one has any mice. We could cite hundreds of examples of engineers who had a "build it, and they will come" attitude only to be rudely awakened by an indifferent market. But it's not just technology companies. Ninety-five percent of all new products don't last more than a few years in the market, but at least consumer goods companies tend to appreciate the value of marketing. (In a very famous episode in the history of American business, Steve Jobs hired a big gun from Pepsi to be the CEO of Apple. He did so because of the man's understanding of the importance of marketing.) In our experience, technology companies are on the leading edge of the overwhelming majority of companies who don't "get" marketing. No matter what your business or industry, we want to make sure that you don't make the same mistake.

I. The Anatomy of a Sale

Let's start by looking at a simple anatomy of a sale. It complements the Four Pillars we will be deep drilling on later. Look at the Marketing Funnel called AIDA below. Here, AIDA stands for Attention, Interest, Desire. (Aida is also a famous opera by Verdi, and it is also a musical by Elton John.) The funnel is often represented by the following picture. You will notice that the funnel is wider at the top than the bottom.

The AIDA Marketing Funnel

- Grab their **Attention**

- Build their **Interest**

- Create the **Desire**

- Persuade them to take **Action**

Another way to look at the above is that Attention represents *Opening the Sale* and Action is *Closing the Sale*. Here the "Sale" could be opting into an email list, making a phone call, redeeming a coupon, making a donation to charity, or purchasing something. What we call the "sales cycle," or how long it takes to go from Opening to Closing, could be an instant or even a year. It takes very little thought to purchase a bag of potato chips that is on sale at 50% off, but signing a contract for a multi-million enterprise software application involving thousands of users is a considerably more complex decision. One issue all marketers face is getting people to buy now rather than later. And of course, some people who come into your funnel will never move through it, meaning that they will never take the action you desire. You can't be all things to all people, despite what you may think.

If you are a well-known celebrity like Tiger Woods or Julia Roberts, you don't have to work very hard to command an audience. Imagine that Tiger sends out a Tweet that he is giving private golf lessons or Julia tells the press that she is conducting acting classes for a dozen people. You can bet that a huge number of those who hear about these offers are going to pay Attention. They may already be in the market for those services, or they may have a remote interest. When people with such visibility and credibility (two prerequisites for success) speak, people listen.

On the other hand, there are those like the rest of us who may be known in our immediate circle but virtually unknown to a wider audience. Our job may be much harder than celebrities and public personalities, but that doesn't mean we can't be successful in getting our message out. Don't forget; everyone starts out as a nobody. We've all heard of people who come out of nowhere and become household names. Television programs such as Canada's Got Talent or American Idol make stars out of virtual unknowns.

Getting someone's Attention is not easy in an age of inundation and clutter. Not everyone in the general population will even notice you or your message even though it might be staring them in the face. Statistics indicate that someone needs to see an ad eight times before showing any Interest whatsoever. It does not mean that they are ready to buy, but they have moved beyond the mere curiosity stage. You may have barely Opened the Sale, but not a whole lot more.

Some of those who pay Attention will have an Interest in what you are saying, moving them one step down the marketing funnel. They may stop for a moment to consider your message. A portion of these people will Desire what you have to sell or offer. And a portion of those who show Desire will move to the narrow end of the funnel and take the Action you wish them to take. You have Closed the Sale with those who comply with your request, whatever it may be.

Let's look at the example of an ad for the luxury automobile Lexus. If it is put along a highway, practically everyone driving by will see it. But some people will be looking in the other direction, so it won't capture everyone's Attention. Anyone who sees the ad will notice the barely-clothed woman. They may even see the headline and the car. The image of the woman is, of course, designed to enhance the appeal of the car. Perhaps it will be sexier in the viewer's estimation if a gorgeous woman is standing in front of it.

Some people paying Attention will have an Interest in the Lexus, but if a person just bought a new luxury car, they are not going to move too far down the funnel. A portion of those who have an Interest will also have the Desire to own the Lexus. But not everyone wants a luxury car, and there are many other brands besides Lexus to choose from.

It is difficult to tell from the tiny print above whether this ad has a specific "Call to Action," but much advertising does not and is simply intended to increase brand awareness or build brand equity. No action is asked for or required. But if a headline screams "Holiday Sale" and the price is temporarily slashed, some people may take Action and go to the dealer to buy before the sale ends. People can be prompted to act if they think they are getting a good deal.

Most of us can't afford brand advertising or advertising that simply gets our name in front of the public. We need to be engaged in advertising that is designed to move people to Action. As a business person, you need to figure out a way to give people reasons to buy now rather than later. You can't afford to engage in messaging that has no purpose other than to be seen.

Chances are if ads contain a picture of an attractive female, more people will pay Attention. The use of the female picture in the ad above helps explain the phrase "sex sells." Sex in advertising is a subject that by itself could take up an entire book, but for our purposes, let's take it for granted that having a scantily clad woman like the one in the Lexus ad is likely to get more people to look. But not all advertisers want to engage in what some would call "cheap and tawdry thrills." Can you imagine an insurance company like Sun Life or Prudential using barely-clothed Victoria's Secret models to sell their products and services? I doubt it.

Fiat ad from the 1950's. The use of attractive women in advertising is still widespread today.

Overview of the Four Pillars

Now that we have looked at how people move through a simple sales funnel, using the four AIDA stages let's go through a brief overview of the pillars and how they are meant to work together as an integrated whole.

The Four Pillars of Business Success

1. Message   2. Market   3. Merchandise   4. Media

1. Message is all about what you say to your target market. It's about communicating your unique value and why your offer solves a specific problem. Hopefully, the problem you solve is an urgent one, like a toothache or a leaking roof. If you're a dentist or a roofer, and the people you serve aren't in any kind of pain, then you're not going to be very busy.

2. Market is the group of people who are your ideal prospects. You may want to think of everyone as a potential buyer, but few companies have the mass market of a company like Coca-Cola. (On the other hand, even ordinary soft drinks don't appeal to people who have a sugar problem.) The legendary copywriter Gary Bencivenga made the observation that problems are markets. Take that to heart. There is a lot of talk about segmentation, demographics, psychographics, and

statistics, but this type of profiling has its limitations. When you think about it, everyone who has a specific problem can be considered part of the target market for that solution. Young or old, rich or poor, when you have a broken arm, you are in need of a doctor. (As we said before, there are a lot of business books that describe all kinds of ways of understanding and categorizing your markets. Some are useful, but much is overkill for those with limited time on their hands and limited budgets. "What problem do you solve" is something that needs to be asked by all of us, and answering it effectively will prevent many a disaster.

3. Merchandise means your product or service and the offers you put together. You can have a physical product, such as a watch or car, or something less tangible like expertise or advice. Even if you offer consulting, training, or coaching services, you would do well to learn merchandising techniques used by retailers. They have the resources to test many variables to see what works and what doesn't. Even though tastes may change, you need to determine how to package and price what you offer so that it appeals to others.

4. Media refers to the way you get your message into your target market. How are you reaching out to others? What media outlets are you using? There are hundreds of ways to communicate with your audience, some of them free, others paid. Advertising, which is a paid form of communication, is often an effective method of attracting the attention of your target market. A lot of companies try to build their business without investing in advertising, and a lot of advertising is certainly wasted or ineffective, but "pay to play" can vault your business to the top in short order. There is a reason why companies pay millions for a Super Bowl ad. Social media, which started out as mostly free, has evolved to the point that you can

buy advertising on platforms such as Facebook, YouTube, and Twitter.

We mentioned that the Four Pillars need to work together as an integrated whole. You can have the greatest Merchandise in the whole world, but if you can't effectively communicate the Message of why someone might want to buy it, you are going to be left behind. You can be a master of Media, but if your announcement is showing up in the wrong places at the wrong times, your ideal target Market isn't going to see it. Many billions of dollars have been wasted on advertising to people who aren't interested, aren't qualified, and aren't ready to act upon whatever is being promoted. With Pay Per Click, it is easier than ever to throw money down the drain by overbidding for keywords or displaying poor landing pages. (Actually, the money isn't going down the drain – it is going into the coffers of Google, Microsoft, and other publishers who will happily take an advertiser's money even though the ads have no chance of working as intended.)

Ideally, your Message will be aimed at the right Market with the right offer of Merchandise through the right Media at the Right Time so that people respond to any Call to Action you might have. A concept popularized by Dan Kennedy is "Message to Market Match." You want to make sure that the two are in sync. In other words, you don't want to be advertising real estate seminars to people who are really interested in beating the stock market.

Now don't get the idea that success is guaranteed by having all Four Pillars working in harmony. The Right Time mentioned above is critical. You can't sell to all people, and timing is critical. If someone has just bought a new car, they are unlikely to need another. In the Chapter called

Techniques of Persuasion, we will examine the variable of time and related factors such as urgency and scarcity later. There are ways to offer incentives that get people to act now rather than later, some heavy-handed and even manipulative, others entirely ethical and transparently persuasive. The word Free has extreme value, for example. Who wouldn't want a Free Ticket to the Super Bowl? Or the chance to win a Free Car?

At the end of this book, we will look at several classic advertisements that embody the best in integrating the Four Pillars. We will spend some time analyzing ads that have been at the foundation of creating or rescuing billion dollar businesses. Because their Messages were in tune with their chosen Markets with offers of Merchandise being shown in the appropriate Media, these ads were able to move people to action. Not all of them were selling anything directly from the ad, it should be noted. Some of them were of the direct response variety, which has the intention of having the reader respond immediately to a Call to Action. But others were designed to educate or to create a lasting impression upon the reader's mind. In all cases, however, the ultimate aim was to foster business success or to sell.

II. Pillar One: Message

Pillar One, the first critical foundation for your business, is your Message. Whether you offer products or services, your business starts with what you say and how you say it. You need to communicate using the tools of words, numbers, and images. In our view, the most important communications tool you have is the word, as it is the underpinning of your story. Even if you are primarily a visual communicator, words are often at the foundation of your story.

Research shows that each of us is exposed to about 3,000 sales messages a day. Most of them we don't even notice. Every car, for example, has an emblem that can be considered advertising. On any given day, we see these advertisements for Toyota, Hyundai, Mercedes, BMW, and Nissan. Your computer has the logo of the manufacturer featured prominently on the cover or elsewhere, often positioned so that others besides the user are reminded of the brand. For example, note how the word "Toshiba" is engraved onto the computer's cover in the photo below. Obviously, the logo has been placed so that anyone walking by will see the brand Toshiba. You may not have thought of the placement of a logo on a computer cover as a form of advertising, but the people at Toshiba certainly do.

Toshiba Computer – with Open Cover

The radio and television are full of ads. And the Internet is full of advertising. We can't possibly keep track of all the ads we see, so most pass us by without our giving them a second thought. To keep our sanity, we can only allow a few into our consciousness. If you are like most consumers, your mailbox is full of unsolicited (junk) mail. You receive phone calls from telemarketers. Your inbox is full of emails all screaming out for attention. Only a chosen number will be opened, and fewer will be acted upon. Everywhere you turn, you are bombarded with advertising and other solicitations that are trying to overcome your natural tendency to reject the unknown.

Clutter, inundation, and time scarcity are characteristics of our modern world. We are constantly rushing from one activity to another, and finding the time to relax or even think is difficult. Taking time to "smell the roses" has become more difficult than ever. Marketers face an uphill challenge in being heard above the ever-increasing noise.

How do you cut through the clutter? As a marketer, you have only a few tools at your disposal, no matter how much money you have to spend. (If money were the only criterion for success, all well-funded companies would be successful. But they're not.) In order to cut through the clutter, you need to be a master at employing a few principles.

Let's start with words. They have never been more important in getting past the chaos and overwhelm that we find ourselves immersed in. Words and how they are delivered are your most valuable tools for standing out from the crowd. If you don't know how to construct effective messages and ensure that they resonate with the emotional brains of your targets, you are doomed to failure. Either you will be ignored, or you will be swimming in what someone calls "a sea of sameness." People need to see a reason to prefer you and your offering over other possibilities.

When you meet some new, here are some typical questions you might encounter:

- Who are you?
- What's your story?
- What's so great about your company?
- What's so great about your offering?
- Why should I buy from you?
- Why should I buy from you now?
- How are you different from others?
- How are you better?
- What's your Unique Selling Proposition? (or Unique Value Proposition, etc.)

If you are promoting your business and someone asks you what you do, you need very compelling answers that focus on the listener, not on you and how great you are. As Chet Holmes said, you are the Producer, and what you think doesn't matter. What's important is what the Consumer thinks. If they don't like what you are saying, you are in trouble. You can't just focus on yourself and ignore what you can do for them. You must show benefits to the recipient.

Let's say you are a photographer and that someone asks you about yourself. Compare the following responses:

A. I am a photographer, and I studied at the Great School of Photography.

B. I take photographs that make people shine and look their best.

The first "product oriented" response is boring, flat, and far too typical. "I am a kitchen designer," "I am a wellness coach," and "I am a math tutor" pale in comparison to "I design beautiful layouts in the most important room in your house," "I help people live happier and healthier," and "I help people overcome their math phobia so they can excel on college entrance exams and get into Harvard."

Yet the vast majority of us focus on what we do. Go to a dozen websites and look at what they say. Ask people about their business. Almost invariably it's about them, not about you. We speak about the "great widgets" we make or "excellent customer service" and "commitment to quality," as if those separate us from others. They don't.

Imagine you are given an opportunity to say something to everyone. You want to make sure that what you say is coherent and that your delivery resonates with your audience. You don't want just to stumble and bumble your way through muddled phrases that are entirely forgettable.

Your Message is the Key to Your Success.
In Business, Silence is Not Golden

Here is a template for explaining to people why you do

what you do. The words in **bold italics** show that you must offer a solution to a problem that others have. You have done something that they have yet to do, which makes you a hero in their eyes. The bigger the solution, the more substance your business will have. If you find a cure for a type of cancer that afflicts millions, you are going to have more demand than if you find a cure that only a few thousand people need. And you will be rewarded accordingly.

Proven Formula for "Why I Do What I Do"

1. Ask a question that involves a **problem**.

2. State one or two sentences showing how you **struggled** with that **problem.**

3. Note a **turning point** in your life where you **solved** the problem.

4. Tell what happened **next.**

5. Say, "And now I can help you **overcome** that same **problem** if … **you send me money, contribute to my charity, buy my product, etc**.

One example:

"Do you suffer from diabetes? For many years, I did too. Then I decided to go to medical school just so I could tackle this all-too-common problem. Late one night, working in my laboratory, I found a cure. It was the miraculous end to a long journey. Clinical trials show that it works. And now I can help you conquer diabetes if you take my new drug."

The Universal Framework of the Hero's Journey

"There are only two or three human stories, and they keep repeating themselves as fiercely as if they had never happened before."   *- Willa Cather*

Although there is no one "right answer" to "Why do you do what you do?", the above template fits into a proven framework known as the Hero's Journey. First popularized by Joseph Campbell in his landmark book **The Hero with a Thousand Faces**, Campbell found that that myths and legends throughout time and across cultures shared a common theme. Campbell divided the Hero's Journey into 17 separate stages, as shown in the following diagram.

We won't get into the details here, but the Hero's Journey or its female equivalent, the Heroine's Journey, has been told in endless ways and continues to capture our imagination. Going counter clockwise the journey starts with Refusal of Call and ends with Freedom to Live. There are three core elements of the Journey – the Hero, the Obstacle, the Treasure – are the same elements at work in the "Why I Do What I Do" formula. You became heroic by solving a problem, and those in your target market view you as heroic. Moreover, they see themselves as being heroic by buying into what you offer. In a nutshell, they are following in your heroic footsteps when they too solve the problem that you have already solved.

Star Wars

No movie has captured our imaginations like Star Wars, the seventh installment of which was released at the end of 2015. Little known is that in the 1970's creator George Lucas hired Joseph Campbell to consult on the script for the first movie. The two used the archetype of the Hero's Journey as the glue that holds the story together. We have the mentor, tricksters, aides, heroes, villains, and many more characters that make up the Hero's Journey. The Belly of the Whale (Stage 5), a reference to the Biblical Jonah, is recreated in the trash compactor scene. Viewers may not get the Biblical allusion, but the feeling of trying to free oneself from a trap is universal.

Star Wars has become a multi-billion-dollar franchise, and The Force Awakens is setting box office records. Lucas openly credits the Hero's Journey archetype as critical to its success, and we see similar tales of heroism in other movies, novels, and in real life.

The Importance of a Powerful Unique Selling Proposition (USP)

Many, if not most businesses do not differentiate themselves from others in the market. Or it they do, they don't ensure that the ways they are different appeal to their target market. All too often there is a message-to-market mismatch.

Jay Abraham suggests that "Most businesses do not have a USP. [They have] only a me too, rudderless, nondescript, unappealing business that feeds solely upon the sheer momentum of the marketplace. There's nothing unique; there's nothing distinct. They promise no great value, benefit, or service—just 'buy from us' for no justifiable, rational reason."

Consider the following descriptions of actual businesses. Do they make you want to contact them? Is there anything about them that stands out?

1. [Name Hidden] has developed expertise in providing general counsel services to business and life coaches nationwide. He has a program to assist them with their internal corporate documents, contracts with clients, joint venture agreements with other coaches, media rights agreements at live events and other intellectual property agreements.

2. [Name Hidden], MBA is the award-winning CEO of [Name], LLC, a business optimization consulting firm that specializes in helping various stage entrepreneurs and business owners master brand messaging, sales, marketing, and operations. She is a sought-after speaker, best-selling author, certified business and executive coach and a lover of helping women step into their divine gifts and talents that change lives and solve problems

We think you will agree that there is no compelling USP at work in either of the above. They're about as boring as could be. We could probably find a thousand people who do what they do and promise what they promise.

A powerful USP can be the foundation of a billion-dollar

business. FedEx and Domino's Pizza are two examples of businesses that were founded on completely new benefits that customers found attractive. FedEx made overnight delivery practically a must-have, and Domino's guaranteed fast delivery even though their pizza wasn't even close to high quality. Let's face it, a lot of people ordering pizza simply want something good to eat, not a meal of the finest quality. (Papa John's Pizza has made a name for itself with "Better Ingredients. Better Pizza" as its slogan. They are targeting a different crowd compared to Domino's.)

Here are some companies and their USPs or slogans:

FedEx "When it Absolutely, Positively Has to Be There Overnight"

Domino's Pizza "Fresh hot pizza delivered in 30 minutes or it's free"

Amazon Prime "Free 2-Day Shipping"

Walmart "Always Low Prices. Always."

Mercedes-Benz "The Best or Nothing"

TD Canada Trust "Banking Can Be This Comfortable."

L'Oréal "Because You're Worth It".

Notice how each USP or slogan is very specific. People know what to expect. There is none of the mushy and vague sentiment such as "great customer service" or "high quality" or "we believe in excellence" that is so prevalent in the market. People know what to expect, which weeds out people who don't qualify or who seek benefits that you don't offer. If you aren't interested in driving the best car (or an approximation), you won't even look at Mercedes. L'Oréal, which caters to older women who want a quality product, appeals to their sense of entitlement. *You deserve the best,* they proclaim. *Don't settle for cheap drugstore cosmetics.* Considering that this campaign has been on the air for many years, it is obviously working. Women know where L'Oréal stands in the market and don't confuse the company with Maybelline or Avon. As we said, a good USP is unique.

USP's should be formulated through research and testing. Clients, partners, employees, and others who know your company and the competition can provide valuable insights on how they view your company's uniqueness. Once a USP is decided upon, it needs to be woven into the fabric of the organization. It must then be spread throughout the company's customers, prospects, partners, and others who can influence the market. When a USP works, everyone, both internal and external to the company, knows exactly what makes the company unique. Review the USPs and slogans for FedEx, Walmart, and L'Oréal above. There is no doubt about where these companies are positioned in the marketplace.

Here are some guidelines about what makes a USP work.

Keys to Blockbuster USPs

- ▶ USPs are not always the same as Slogans. They are often more comprehensive.
- ▶ USPs are not fixed. They evolve.
- ▶ USPs can be based on the hidden assets that *already exist* in your business.
- ▶ USPs appeal to both emotions and logic.
- ▶ USPs must fill a market desire (known and unknown)
- ▶ USPs are formulated as a result of a structured process. They take time and effort to create and discover/uncover.

▸ USPs must be backed up by compelling PROOF

▸ *USPs are benefit-driven, bold, memorable, overt, quantitative.*

▸ *USPs can be the foundation of a billion-dollar business.*

How to Make Your Advertising Memorable

In this book, you're going to get a look at some of the most successful ads in history. But more importantly, we will dissect them and examine what makes them so effective. As Jay Abraham says, "human nature is immutable." The same hopes, dreams, and fears that humans had decades ago are the same ones they have today.

There is no need for you to reinvent the wheel when you create your own messages. You need to study what has worked in the past and then adapt it to your own unique situation. To paraphrase T.S. Eliot, "immature poets imitate; mature poets steal; bad poets deface what they take, and good poets make it into something better, or at least something different." In other words, use what is available but make it your own. Borrow, but don't plagiarize.

If you haven't heard of a Swipe File, it's a collection of great copywriting that someone has swiped from other sources. Very often it will contain a template or two, something like "Paint by Numbers." Your swipe file can serve as an inspiration for your own copy, even if you flunked English.

Once you have your USP put together, you can infuse your advertising (and other forms of messaging such as blogs, emails, social media posts, etc.) with it and stand out from the crowd. We should reinforce that advertising is a tried-and-true method of getting your message out into the world. If you rely on free traffic and word-of-mouth, or any form of "hope marketing," you don't have a viable business. SEO algorithms can change in a heartbeat as many a marketer had found when Google made modifications that caused traffic of many a merchant to slow to a trickle. Overnight million dollar businesses went bankrupt.

If you followed the mandate that your USP be UNIQUE, then no one else does what you do, at least not in your target market. (It is obviously hard for a dry cleaner to be different from all other dry cleaners on earth, but you can certainly be different from those in a 10-mile radius. One local dry cleaner I know gives a 40% discount if items are left for 7 days. A lot of people aren't in a hurry, and they take advantage of such a USP.) The headline of any ad is its most important written feature. If a reader is not captivated by the headline, chances are he or she will not read the rest of the copy.

How to Write a Good Headline

John E. Kennedy once defined advertising as "Salesmanship in Print." He wrote in an era before the computer, but his fundamentals of communication still hold true today. In print, the most important part of an ad is the headline. We will analyze John Caples' classic ad "They Laughed When I Sat Down at the Piano." This headline is considered one of the greatest of all time.

The purpose of the headline is to have the reader go on to the next part of the ad. Without a good headline, people won't engage with the body of the text. Caples wrote a classic book called **Tested Advertising Methods** that is still studied today.

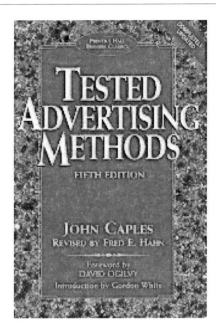

Writing headlines (and body copy) may seem to be simple, but there is a lot of thought and analysis that goes creating ones that last. In addition, what the copywriter thinks of a good headline may not be what the market thinks. Here are some guidelines from **Tested Advertising Methods** for writing good headlines.

1. Begin your headline with the word "Announcing"
2. Use words that have an announcement quality
3. Begin your headline with the word "New"
4. Begin your headline with the word "Now"
5. Begin your headline with the word "At Last"
6. Put a date into your headline
7. Write your headline in news style
8. Feature the price in your headline
9. Feature reduced price
10. Feature a special merchandising offer
11. Feature an easy-payment plan
12. Feature a free offer
13. Offer information of value

14. Tell a story
15. Begin your headline with the words "How to"
16. Begin your headline with the word "How"
17. Begin your headline with the word "Why"
18. Begin your headline with the word "Which"
19. Begin your headline with the word "Who Else"
20. Begin your headline with the word "Wanted"
21. Begin your headline with the word "This"
22. Begin your headline with the word "Advice"
23. Use a testimonial-style headline
24. Offer the reader a test
25. Use a one-word headline
26. Use a two-word headline
27. Warn the reader to delay buying
28. Let the manufacturer speak directly to the reader
29. Address your headline to a specific group or person

The headline is often said to account for 80% of the effectiveness of an ad. It serves the same function as a book title and is designed to make the reader want to continue reading. Ted Nicholas once said that he would write 400 different headlines before eventually narrowing the choice down to one. He would use the best of the unused headlines as bullets in a multi-page sales letter. Anyone who thinks that copywriting is easy has obviously never done it well.

III. Pillar Two: Market

The second pillar has to do with understanding your Market, the people who are your ideal prospects and eventual buyers. You may want to think of everyone as a potential customer, but few companies have the mass market of a company like Coca-Cola. (On the other hand, even they don't sell to people who have a sugar problem.) Gary Bencivenga taught the idea that problems are markets. Take that to heart. There is a lot of thinking around segmentation, demographics, psychographics, and statistics, but when you think about it, everyone who has a specific problem can be considered part of the target market for that solution.

Young or old, rich or poor, if you have a broken arm, you are in need of a doctor. If you have a toothache, you want to see a dentist. It doesn't matter whether you are single or married, white or black. (As we said before, there are a lot of business books that describe all kinds of ways of understanding and categorizing your markets. Some are useful, but much is overkill for marketers with limited time on their hands and limited budgets.)

"What problem do you solve?" is something that needs to be asked by all of us who are in business. Answering it effectively will prevent many a disaster. Don't think that your solution will find an audience without adequate testing. Someone we know burned through $50 million in funding and later reminisced ruefully, "People didn't care about the problem I was solving. I couldn't make the market want what it didn't want." It is a mistake to think that a better mousetrap is a guarantee of success. Many great products have failed, whereas many lesser ones have succeeded. Better marketing can often compensate for an inferior product.

One blunder that is all too common is that a company wants to sell what it produces rather than what the market will buy. Products are often developed by engineers and designers with precious little input from actual buyers. As a result, the failure rate of new products is extremely high, with some estimates at 95%. In other words, 1 in 20 products succeeds, whereas the rest fail. Even if there is a perceived desire for what we offer, our messaging or packaging may not fit what the market wants to hear.

Understanding Your Target Market

The better you can understand your ideal buyer the easier time you will have in delivering specific messages that they will respond to. Demographic attributes such as income levels and where people live are only partially useful. For example, there are people who make a million dollars or more in many lower income towns. If you offer a Mercedes-like product, you will miss many potential buyers if you market only by geography. Besides external factors such as home values, occupation, age, and income, you need to understand buyer behavior, values, lifestyle, preferences, and the like. Even people who own BMW's shop at Wal-Mart in order to save money. They may like the convenience of McDonald's even though they could afford a $20 lunch. They may also shop at Tiffany's for expensive jewelry and generic, low-priced gasoline.

What do your buyers value? Low price or high quality? Off the rack clothing or tailored outfits? The convenience of a corner store or the maze-like layout of a big box retailer? A vast selection of brand-name merchandise or a narrow range of choices among premium brands? You must know who your buyer is and how to find them.

Pillar Two: Market

To better understand your prospect, here are some questions you should answer:

- What kinds of people will be interested in your offering?
- What are their professional and personal interests?
- What are their hobbies?
- What keeps your prospects up at night?
- What are the buying criteria your prospect uses to evaluate possible purchases?
- What are the buyer pain points in relation to what you offer?
- Where do your buyers congregate – online and offline?
- What types of clubs, societies, charities, and groups do your prospects belong to?

If you sell to businesses, you want to know attributes such as the following:

- Company size – employees, locations, etc.
- Industry and sub-industry
- Revenue
- Profitability
- Growth rate
- Buyer and influencer titles
- Buyer departments
- Purchasing criteria
- Competitor product or service used
- Readiness to adopt

Buyer Psychology

There is an old saying, "people buy on emotion and justify with logic." It may take many years of hearing this to get used to this way of looking at things. We love to think that we are rational and that our decision-making is based on reason and logic, not passion and emotion. Modern economics was founded on the idea of perfect markets and complete rationality, and actual human behavior was given little consideration. Much of our training focuses on the "hard facts" and "numbers," leaving little room for an understanding of the emotional landscape of the target buyer. But the tide is slowly turning.

Many of us think that because we are logical in our presentation of the benefits and features of our offering that the person hearing our message is receiving it through the thinking mind. In fact, they are not. Neuroscience has shown that new information is filtered through the emotional mind, where it is either allowed to travel to the thinking mind or tossed aside as irrelevant and unwanted. The entire process could take place in a nanosecond, but the point here is that we do not receive information through the part of the brain that processes language, math, and logic. Our messages, therefore, must have emotional appeal above all else or it will be rejected. The emotional brain is the primitive part of the brain and has a gut response to new information. If messages are too complex or require too much thought to digest, they will have a hard time getting past the lower brain to get a hearing from the higher brain.

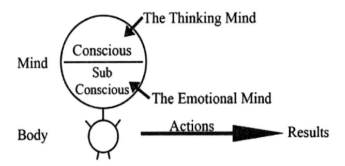

**Information is received and filtered by the Emotional Mind.
Whatever is not rejected is passed through to the Thinking Mind.**

Market tests and research studies have shown that the emotional mind, the lower part of the brain, is actually in more control of what we do than we would like to admit. The higher brain neocortex is a recent development in evolution, and despite our highly-developed logical capabilities, people are largely driven by the unconscious. If someone yells "fire" in a crowded theater, you aren't going to stop and ask what kind of fire – you are going to scramble for the exits and then sort the matter out later.

As marketers, we must be aware that people are driven by emotions such as fear, greed, jealousy, envy, pain, pleasure, and revenge as well as more rational considerations such as quality, price, selection, value, and benefit. If you have ever been motivated to take advantage of a special offer before the time limit ran out, you have engaged in behavior related to the Fear of Missing Out (FOMO). Many a sale has been engineered using various scarcity tactics that we will examine in Chapter six.

IV. Pillar Three: Merchandise

The third pillar is Merchandise. Our use of the word here goes far beyond the physical goods that we normally refer to as merchandise. Besides tangible things, it also means services in the broadest sense, ranging from accounting services to legal advice to consulting. The word also takes into account both WHAT you offer and HOW you offer it. Taking a cue from the retail industry, you need to think about your offerings as a type of merchandise even if they are purely service oriented and "intangible."

If you have followed the guidelines we presented in Pillars One and Two, your merchandise has to fill a desire in the market. You must know or be able to determine that there is a demand for what you offer or that you can take existing demand and direct it your way. In Domino's case, they took an ordinary industry – pizza – and created a business based on fast delivery. For Domino's, "merchandise" included a delivery promise, not just a pizza. In the case of the iPad, Apple took the tablet – which had been around for years – and turned it into something revolutionary. The iPhone married the cell phone with a computer and turned it into much more than either one alone.

Whether you are inventing a new category, refining an existing category, or simply building a better mousetrap with a novel approach, you must ensure that a large enough population is willing to buy it or you won't have a business. Of course, this is easier said than done. Otherwise, the failure rate of new businesses wouldn't be so great.

One mistake marketers often make, is thinking that people will change behavior in order to buy what they are offering. If your product falls into the category of something they are already buying, then you are looking for a share of an already existing market. Buyers are already looking for a solution like yours, and you can attract attention by being unique. This is by far the easiest approach. For example, if you offer a new accounting software solution, you are entering an existing market and don't need to change existing behavior in any significant way.

But if your item is not already on their buying list, then your job is likely to be much harder. You need to engage in what is called "market development," often a difficult task. Today's personal computer is commonplace, but for years, computer companies struggled to find buyers. Many a pioneering company tried and failed to build a lasting company, for a variety of reasons. Osborne had a lock on portable computers at one time, but they disappeared along with dozens of early entrants. In persuading consumers to change existing behavior, you are looking for them to spend money in a new area.

If you are selling to a company, this would mean that they would have to add a new line item in their budget. Buyers need to be educated on the need for something entirely new, and they may resist change. And if your solution is complex and requires lots of persuasion and convincing as to why they should buy it, your job is even tougher. This is not to say that it can't be done. Let's not forget that every truly new product category did not exist at one time. Many items we now call commonplace took years or even decades for adoption to be widespread.

Trying to change behavior is one of the toughest jobs in the world. We have already seen that the emotional brain plays an integral role in the decision-making process, and it doesn't want to think too hard. It would rather be left alone. Asking it to entertain new ideas and weigh cost-benefit trade-offs in a new product category is asking a lot. Many a company has run out of time and money trying to "change the world," only to find out that the world isn't particularly interested in change. The only person who likes change is a baby with a wet diaper. If the market doesn't perceive the need for a change, no amount of convincing will do.

You also need to think of how you package your merchandise when you offer it to the market. Packaging is used here to mean much more than physical packaging. For example, you may charge $1500 for a day of consulting, but if someone asks for a week of your services, you may charge less than the $7500 "retail" amount. If you sell widgets that cost $10 each, you may sell two for less than $20 in order to give people an incentive to purchase more than one. Buy One Get One Free, also known as BOGO, has become a staple of many merchandisers. A BOGO sale amounts to 50% off when you buy two. We want you to think as merchandisers when you look at what you offer. Discounts, trial periods, layaway plans, bonuses, and hundreds of other tactics are used to encourage customers to buy now rather than later.

As we said at the beginning of this book, price and volume are the two elements you can manipulate to your heart's content in order to drive revenue. Smart marketers know that some buyers are price sensitive and will buy more when prices are lowered. Both businesses and consumers are motivated to get a good deal. If a company such as Staples has a Thanksgiving Sale where many computers are 1/3 off, a lot of people will stand in line for hours to save a few hundred dollars. On the other hand, there may not be much of an effect on demand when the price of a car is raised from $52,000 to $53,000 or lowered from $53,000 to $52,000. Economists and marketers gauge the effects of "price elasticity" to determine optimal prices that maintain the desired balance among inventory, sales, profit, and other variables.

Your offer must be compelling and easy to understand. If not, it has no chance of being irresistible, which is one goal of the marketer. Offering a new car at 75% off will be irresistible to some. Marketers often overly complicate matters by making their offers confusing, full of jargon, and hard to decipher. They will use 10 words when 3 will do, filling the prospect's brain with too much information. Or they will provide too many choices, making the buying decision difficult. One study found that a supermarket that displays 30 jams to be sampled resulted in far fewer sales than displaying only 6 jars. One might think that having more choice would result in more sales, but this was not the case. The confused mind never buys.

Several marketers have used the phrase "you'd have to be an idiot not to take me up on this offer," loading their offer with massive benefits and advantages. Some will buy, but others, especially those who are not in the target market, will move on. This underscores the importance of matching the merchandise to the right market. If I don't have a headache, even the best aspirin in the world at an attractive price isn't going to sway me.

Why Services Businesses Need to Offer Products

Advertising agencies have long maintained that their assets go out the door every evening. They are referring to their employees as assets, as an agency sells creativity, ingenuity, innovation, and strategy. Unlike product-driven companies, advertising agencies, consultants, lawyers, doctors, accountants, and countless other service businesses often sell themselves by a unit of time. An hour of time costs a certain amount, and multiple hours cost more. The obvious problem with a time-based business is that there are only 24 hours in a day. Even if you charge $1000 per hour, the most you can make in one day without taking a break is $24,000.

With a product business, the amount you can earn in one day is in theory unlimited. The allure of "making money while you sleep" goes out the window if there is no packaged offering that anyone can buy at any time whether it is a book, software application, car, or another kind of "widget." The Internet has made shopping for goods much easier than before, and now many stores never close. Any company that can manufacture more of its products can always sell more.

But no one has yet figured out how to manufacture time. If a time-driven business is going to go beyond "trading time for money," it would do well to think of ways it can offer products that can be sold like widgets.

V. Pillar Four: Media

How you get your message into the market will have a major impact on your success. In today's world, the possibilities for making your presence known have never been greater. This is both an advantage and a disadvantage. If you are the only one talking, people will listen. If you are competing with millions for the attention of a few, the job is more difficult.

Years ago, when television was first introduced, there were only a few commercial channels. The number grew with the addition of different frequencies until cable and satellite exploded the number of available channels into the hundreds. The introduction of the Internet gave everyone the opportunity to put up their own website, and today there are hundreds of millions of sites vying for attention. It seems that everyone has something to say, no matter how important or trivial.

More recently, the availability of social media outlets and news sites have mushroomed to the point where it seems that news is found everywhere, from Tweets that pass in the wind or Facebook postings that scroll by as fast as you can read them. Filtering out the important from the irrelevant has almost become a full-time occupation. In other words, the clutter problem has gotten worse than ever.

On the other hand, what hasn't changed is the 24-hour day, as we noted before in another context. No one has yet figured out how to give us more time to deal with the ever-increasing amount of information. And our lives have become busier than ever. Few of us can say that life has become simpler with the continuous technological change that gives us more and more gadgets and devices to deal with.

As you determine where and how to get your message out, it is important to remember that your target market is going to favor some media above others. If you have properly profiled the behavior of your ideal prospect, you will know a lot about the kind of media they favor. Not all should be treated equally, whether online or offline. Consumers flock to Facebook and Pinterest now, whereas LinkedIn is for professional communication. **New York Times** and **Scientific American** readers differ from **National Enquirer** readers. You need to be intimately familiar with the conversation taking pace in your target's mind and where that conversation is being seen and shared with others. You need to know where your prospect goes – online and offline – for information, relaxation, and the like. If you fit in as a normal part of the conversation, you are much more likely to be welcomed than if you are seen as a spammer or interloper simply selling something.

Many companies that sell to professionals and businesses have the opportunity to join and lead LinkedIn groups, a relatively new phenomenon. No longer are people limited to activities in their local area – they can be seen by a worldwide audience very quickly. Such potential to develop the position of authority or leader opens doors up where they never existed before. There are thousands of special interest groups on LinkedIn that one can join at no charge. Facebook, Twitter, Pinterest and other platforms also give anyone the opportunity to join like-minded groups and be seen as a trusted advisor.

We want you to think of Media in a broad sense and include tried-and-true channels such as word of mouth marketing and referral marketing among the possibilities. There are many ways of getting your message out into the world than relying on the media, paid or unpaid. Network marketing is built upon these two, and enormous companies such as Amway and Herbalife have been created without relying on traditional advertising. Affiliate marketing is another way of gaining reach, a key goal of many marketers. If you can form alliances with key affiliates who have followings of people you are trying to reach, you can expand your customer list very quickly. There is no need to rely only on advertising and your own customer base to build a business.

There are more types of Media than ever to consider as you think about getting your message out. Many have both a paid and non-paid component and an online and offline venue. For example, you can get an article written in a magazine (unpaid) or place an ad there (paid). Some advertisers do both at the same time. And you can post for free and also pay to advertise on Facebook. As we have mentioned, "pay to play" via advertising is a way to ensure that your message gets out into the world. In today's fast-paced world, a free posting or another type of unpaid coverage may disappear without being seen by many viewers. This is not to say that people will read your ad, but advertisers guarantee circulation or proof that your ad appeared.

There are countless types of Media available for you to broadcast or narrowcast your message. There are more than 500 television channels you can advertise on, many of them with a very narrow focus. For example, there are several food-related channels that appeal to food and cooking lovers. If you have a big budget and a wide-ranging offering, you can take out an ad in the Wall Street Journal or USA Today. You can buy national network television time. Most of us need to make do with smaller media or even go the free route. Here are some Media for your consideration. Each has its own characteristics, and your messages need to be adjusted accordingly.

- Affiliates
- Billboards
- Blog Posts
- Brochures and catalogs
- Direct mail
- Discovery sessions
- Editorials
- Email
- Facebook (free and ads
- Joint ventures
- LinkedIn
- Lists
- Magazines
- Newspapers
- Press Releases
- Radio
- Referral partners
- Sales letters
- Sales representatives
- Seminars
- SEO
- Social media
- Speaking
- Sponsoring events
- Television
- Trade shows
- Webinars
- Website
- White papers
- Word of mouth
- YouTube

This list is far from exhaustive, but it will give you a good idea of the myriad of possibilities. Many companies rely solely on channels that are used by others in their industry, whereas innovative ones look beyond their industry to find what may work. Some of the above channels such as Facebook barely existed a few years ago and have now grown into powerhouses. With its 1 billion users, Facebook should be looked at seriously to determine if using it can pay off. If you are not ahead of the curve, you risk being left behind.

No discussion on sales and marketing Media would be complete without a discussion of Google AdWords and related Search Engine Marketing outlets. People around the world perform more than 3 billion searches a day on Google, Yahoo, Bing, and other search engines. That's a lot of searching. Although not for everyone, one reason Google has such a massive stock market valuation is that it allows companies to target their advertising to those most likely to buy in an entirely measurable way. Because of the ability to track results, Google brought direct response marketing, where advertising asks the viewer to take a specific action, back into the mainstream.

Measuring the effectiveness of an ad is a marketer's dream, and Google reduced the process of collecting and analyzing results from months to minutes. Online marketing and advertising, which is distinct from brand marketing, seeks an immediate response from the consumer. Google gives everyone with Internet access a chance to get their message out into the world, allowing someone in the middle of Alberta or Saskatchewan the opportunity to be seen around the world in just a few minutes. Mastering AdWords and Google Analytics are two important online marketing activities, as they allow you to read the mind of your market in ways that were previously impossible.

VI. Techniques of Persuasion

"Find out what people want, then show
them how to get it."
- Bernard Baruch

One of the most important skills anyone can have is that of persuasion. Having someone voluntarily act upon your wishes is a subject that has been endlessly studied. Politicians want your vote. Merchants want your business. Governmental authorities want you to obey the law. Getting someone to agree with you and act upon that agreement is something all of us want, whether it's about which movie to see, what neighborhood to move to, or what time your child is supposed to go to bed.

In essence, persuasion, influence, compliance, adherence, agreement, and the like revolve around questions like "why do people do what they do?" If you can find answers to that question, you can then focus on "how can I influence others to do what I want them to do?" and ultimately "how can I get people to buy what I sell?" This last question is on the mind of every person who is responsible for bringing in sales or making the cash register ring.

In this chapter, we're going to focus on persuasion techniques. We will start with what we will call the honest and above-board ones and then look at some that are a bit distasteful or sleazy. As we go through this chapter, don't forget that well-known marketer Seth Godin wrote a book and titled it **All Marketers Are Liars**. When people got the wrong idea, or some would say the right idea, he changed the title. He crossed out the part about liars and changed the title to **All Marketers Tell Stories**. This, of course, makes marketers and their profession sound much nobler. Who can fault someone for telling stories? No one, unless the stories are tall tales. It is worth noting that Godin did not change his text in any way. People do judge a book by its cover, and the new title was much more friendly to both the author and the reader.

Seth Godin's Revised Book Cover.
The Inside Text Remains Exactly the Same

Thousands of books, reports, articles, and studies have been conducted on human behavior and the art and science of persuasion. Perhaps no person has been so thoroughly immersed in combining the academic side of the subject with the real world as Robert Cialdini, author of **Influence: The Psychology of Persuasion**. If you don't know this book, we suggest you get your hands on it and learn its timeless principles. It is recognized as a classic, yet we are surprised at how many people have yet to hear of it. (Chet Holmes, who worked with Charlie Munger at Berkshire Hathaway, once suggested that only 10% of us learn outside the classroom. This sad statistic helps explain why so many people have yet to benefit from Cialdini's wisdom and the insights of so many others who can help improve business performance. The fact that you are reading this book puts you in the 10% minority. Congratulations.)

Cialdini studied human behavior in the field for many years, focusing on compliance and related subjects. He was fascinated with the many techniques used by those in the compliance professions: salespeople, fundraisers, telemarketers, and solicitors. He even took jobs in sales and fundraising to go through training programs for salespeople and others who had a responsibility to get others to buy, donate, etc.

Although the use of these techniques of influence can and should be an integral part of the Four Pillars we have covered, they are worth calling out separately so that you know how to use them and when and where they are being used on you. Businesses are continually experimenting with every trick in the book and also inventing new tricks to gain compliance from evermore sophisticated consumers, but these principles are fundamental. Here, the notion that there is nothing new under the sun is quite correct.

Cialdini came up with six categories to classify techniques of influence. Each of these has a distinct role in gaining cooperation and can be used independently or together. They are Authority, Consistency, Liking, Reciprocity, Scarcity, and

Social Proof. Here are the definitions in a nutshell:

1. Authority: people tend to comply with the directives of authority figures such as law enforcement, doctors, lawyers, experts, etc.
2. Consistency: people want to act consistently and follow through on their commitments.
3. Liking: people tend to want to associate with others like themselves.
4. Reciprocity: people want to reciprocate when they feel indebted
5. Scarcity: people want what is scarce or what they can't have
6. Social Proof: people follow the actions of others.

Some of the best examples of the above influence techniques are seen in the movie **Catch Me If You Can**, starring Tom Hanks and Leonard DiCaprio. In particular, the way **Authority** is obtained is very instructive. The movie is about the real-life adventures of a con man named Frank Abagnale who later became an FBI consultant. Abagnale, played by DiCaprio, engaged in many deceptions by posing as authority figures like a doctor, a lawyer, and an airline pilot. Anyone who has ever worked in a hospital knows that there is a strict pecking order among the medical staff, with doctors at the top of the food chain. When doctors speak, others listen and obey. And people follow "doctor's orders" sometimes without thinking. In the movie, DiCaprio the doctor has the authority to get others to follow his commands. In real life, Cialdini carried out a series of experiments in hospitals and found that people not associated with a hospital who put on a white coat and called themselves doctors had the ability to persuade nurses to follow orders that violated protocol and strict processes and procedures. Such is the power of a uniform that conveys Authority.

It is also worth noting that among doctors, the length of the white lab coat signifies rank, with trainees wearing shorter coats than experienced doctors. Outsiders can immediately determine who is in charge, and "long coats" command more respect than "short coats." Even within a profession of high authority, there are levels of authority.

When Abagnale poses as a lawyer, he blends right in with those he is conning. The **Liking** principle is at work here, as we tend to associate with those we like. "We do business with those we those we know, like and trust" is a well-worn phrase for good reason. We tend to like those who are like us, not people who don't fit in and who are considered outsiders.

Reciprocity, the principle related to "you scratch my back, and I'll scratch yours," is found everywhere. Fundraisers will often send you a small token of their appreciation such as personalized return address labels in order to induce you into donating. They know that the act of giving first creates a bit of obligation on the recipient's part. Free samples, a staple of supermarket marketing, is designed to instill the same sense of obligation.

Scarcity is another influence technique that has a myriad of applications. Perhaps the Scarcity tactic most often seen involves time. "Buy before it's too late" is seen at work when merchants invented Black Friday, the day after Thanksgiving. It used to be that consumers were expected to line up at the civilized hour of 8 AM to get the best deals at a store, but then the time was moved to 6 AM, then 4 AM, then midnight. Now stores are even open on Thanksgiving Day!

"Limited supply" is another Scarcity technique that has endless applications. It may well be true that there are only a limited number of items produced or seats available – we've all heard about "collector's editions" and "only 500 manufactured, and first come first served." On the other hand, merchants have figured out ways to manipulate consumers into buying more than they might have wanted. Some create a false Scarcity and use gift-giving occasions to line their own pocketbooks at the expense of unsuspecting (that is to say, ignorant) consumers.

One hidden ploy on the part of the toy industry involves Christmas Scarcity. Merchants will heavily advertise specific toys, hoping that little John or Jane will persuade Mom and Dad to buy them as presents. (We hope you realize that toy manufacturers advertise heavily on children's television shows.) Obedient Mom and Dad go to the store, only to find out that there is a shortage of the item in question. They will have to wait until after the holidays to buy the hot new toy. But John and Jane can't go without something, anything, for Christmas, and the parents buy a substitute gift instead.

A few weeks after Christmas, when the excitement of the toy wears off, John and Jane (who are trained to be consumers and to ask their parents for material goods) remember that Mom and Dad promised them the hot new toy. And guess what, they are now readily available at the store. There is no more shortage. The parents, who wish to be consistent with their pre-Christmas promise, are "forced" to buy a second toy in order to satisfy the demands of their children. Parents have fallen into a deliberate trap set for them by the toy industry.

Some might question the ethics of the toy manufacturers whereas others would call their psychological manipulation pure genius. False Scarcity and **Consistency** are being used in order to extract more dollars from consumers. "All's fair in love and war," the saying goes, and there is no doubt that a battle is being waged for your hard-earned dollars. This brings to mind "a fool and his money are soon parted," another well-known phrase. We are not going to go so far as to call consumers fools, but the manipulative tactics being used can be learned. They may be a bit hidden, but a bit of research can uncover them. Once you know about them, you are armed with precious knowledge that allows you to take defensive action. And of course, no one is forcing anyone to buy a second toy. It's not like the manufacturer threatened someone.

The last of the six tactics we will cover here is **Social Proof**. In essence, people follow the herd, and when they see others taking a certain action, they themselves are more likely to take the same action. Casinos hire "shills" to sit at empty blackjack tables since they know that many patrons don't want to play alone. Stores line the tip jars with money at the beginning of the day to suggest that other customers have already tipped. The implication is that you are to follow their lead and not seem cheap. If you see an empty jar, it signals that no one has tipped, so why should you?

Getting people to say "Yes" is a method of signaling Social Proof. At many gatherings, the audience yells out "Yes" in response to a question like, "Are you here to learn how to beat the stock market?" When it is time to buy the "foolproof" way of beating the market, all the Yesses add up make the final Yes more likely. At timeshare sales gatherings, groups of consumers will be asked a series of questions that they respond "Yes" to. If they say "No" when asked to buy, the salesperson will put on a puzzled expression and suggest that all the "Yes" responses are supposed to end up with another

"Yes." The promoter may even have planted a few insiders in the audience whose sole job is to "buy" so that others follow suit.

We first saw the power of Cialdini's principles in action at a seminar in Las Vegas. At an information marketing event in the 1990's with about 500 attendees, speaker after speaker got up on stage over three days and basically proclaimed, "I'm in the Marketing Business. Here's Some Information You Can Use to Grow Your Business. I'm Great. Buy My Stuff." None of the speakers were being paid, so they made their money via back of the room sales. One after another, they all had more or less the same message. "Look at How I've Helped Others Make Money. I'm Great. Buy My Stuff." For most speakers, a handful of people would go to the back after the speech and check out their offerings.

On the afternoon of the third day, someone gave a completely different speech. Instead of telling us how great he was, this speaker used examples from his past to illustrate that point. He engaged in none of the normal "'buy my stuff" pitching. Toward the end of his 45-minute presentation, he made his offer. He said that he was giving two seminars of 21 people each. The limit was 42 people. Participants would learn inside secrets of how to grow an information marketing business. They would also come to his house for dinner and meet his family. He took out 42 $1 bills, saying that each was worth 50% off the normal seminar price of $2,000. Anyone who obtained one of the $1 bills could go to the seminar for only $1,000.

He held the $1 bills over his head in front of 500 people and said, "Come and get it."

And there was a stampede to be one of the fortunate people to get their hands on a $1 bill (and give him $1000 in return). People literally jumped over tables. Within a minute or two, all 42 $1 bills were gone.

The speaker later told us that he architected his speech based on Cialdini's six principles. Every moment of his presentation was choreographed, with Scarcity, Reciprocity, Social Proof, and the other principles carefully illustrated and brought to life during his 45 minutes. His speech worked like a charm, and it was so effective that people in a room of more than 500 jumped over tables.

We mentioned that many of the many techniques marketers employ to gain compliance can be learned in a marketing textbook or book on human behavior. To what extent should consumers cry "foul" if their compliance is due to a marketer's gimmick? To what extent should the consumer be responsible for his or her own behavior? There is no right answer to this question, as the definition of an unfair and deceptive practice is a judgment call.

The Godfather Sales Pitch and Other Related Sales Methods

In the movie **The Godfather,** Marlon Brando wanted to gain someone's cooperation. In a very famous scene, he made an offer that the other person couldn't refuse.

Marlon Brando and his Irresistible Offer in The Godfather

In essence, we want to do the same, although our techniques shouldn't involve intimidation and force. Instead, they should be based on ethical persuasion.

Manipulative selling techniques are commonplace, and they have given salespeople a bad name. We are trained not to trust those in sales, as too often the promise doesn't match the reality. Or there is high pressure put on the prospect. In The Closers Part 1, a best-selling book on sales by Ben Gay III, he tells us that sales is a take-no-prisoners occupation, and he advocates bullying, intimidation, shaming, and a host of other unpleasant tactics in order to win business. Such techniques can and do work, but at what price? Read the following carefully, and remember that it comes from a bestselling book by someone who is at the top of his trade.

In the past writers have maintained a certain level of respect and circumspection toward customers, a respect level that salesmen generally acknowledge and accept. However, in this book no holds are barred. The customer is taken apart and completely dismantled, analyzed and thoroughly examined by the Master Closer. After this dissection, the closer can understand any customer's position. Then the closer, after developing a sound solution, can go in for the kill (the sale).

This book is a straightforward, honest discussion of proven tricks and traps that *do* produce sales. So, if you are really serious about your selling profession, no matter what field of sales you are in, then don't talk to another customer until you have read this book. This book covers virtually every objection from a customer that you will ever encounter. It gives you not only the answers but all the ammunition you will ever need to get the sale that day and keep it solid.

Ben Gay III, The Closers Part 1

Taking customers apart and dismantling them are repugnant tactics you would expect to find in **The Godfather**, not the noble profession of facilitating an exchange between two parties. Such tactics have nothing to do with what we call genuine professionalism.

But wait, there's more, much more. Here are three actual closing techniques found in Gay's book. Gay points out that he is fully aware of the manipulation involved, which is not exactly a ringing endorsement for the sales profession.

The Intimidation Close

DESCRIPTION: This "close" is designed to embarrass and shame the customer into buying the product through pressure and emotions. The closer can be very effective with these "closing statements" if he executes them properly. This kind of "close" has to be used on the customer subtly and tactfully for full effect; if the closer misuses this "closing procedure" he could kill a sale.

The Kids vs. Parents Close

DESCRIPTION: In this "close" the closer uses the excitement and innocence of the customer's children against the customer himself. This close is powerful — in fact it could backfire and kill a sale, but if the closer handles it tactfully and with class the customer won't get too upset, plus he will wind up purchasing the product.

The Three Devil Close

DESCRIPTION: This "close" is great for the older, reserved customer, and especially good for preachers. This "close" actually tells the customer to go to hell when he says he has to think about buying the product. The good thing about this "close" is that the customer won't realize what the closer has just said to him until it's too late to do anything about it. This "close" will absolutely destroy the "I have to think about it" customer.

Please make sure you have read the above very carefully. They are three of twenty closing techniques analyzed, and many others are equally questionable. Although they may work on occasion, many find them distasteful. Embarrassing and shaming prospects or pitting children against parents so that prospects will buy is completely different from what we call ethical persuasion and leading with benefits. For us, sales is not about trickery or deception or anything underhanded.

No wonder there is such resistance to selling and salespeople. We need to be aware that the deck is stacked against us from the start, which makes it all the more important for you to make your messaging important and relevant. If what you say sounds like a sales pitch, defenses will automatically go up. If it is viewed as helpful and informative, it will be received in a much different light. It has a much better chance of getting past the Emotional Mind and being considered by the Thinking Mind.

We advocate transparency in our sales and marketing, but there are others who try to pull the wool over the eyes of others. (This does not mean that we are against using techniques to encourage people to buy, only that one uses them ethically.) For example, there is a mini-industry involved in the manufacture of phony testimonials and then making it appear that they have been seen on the national news or in major outlets such as **The Wall Street Journal** or **Time**. There are a lot of tricks being played out there, much like the tricks and high-pressure techniques Ben Gay openly advertises.

One phony credibility builder that businesspeople pay thousands for is using paid advertising to appear briefly on online sites such as **The New York Times** or a local affiliate of **NBC** or **CBS**. Or they place paid articles on such news sites. The business then features the logos of such media prominently on their website with the intention of making people think they actually received coverage that was initiated by a live editor or reporter. "As Seen on CBS" a headline will scream. We know of many business owners who are all-too-willing to play such games and make it appear that they received real editorial coverage. Instead, all of the publicity was manufactured, and many of the articles never ran on the real online site. We once saw a colleague's website splashed with the following types of logos:

Typical Logos Seen on Websites.
Very Often the Story Behind Them is Not What It Appears to Be

Very often accompanying text says "As Seen On," or "As Featured On." When we inquired about the logos, we found out that our colleague had paid several thousand dollars to a branding outfit simply so they could put these logos on their site without lying completely. The person had never been featured on any of the media outlets – paid advertising that appeared on the media sites for a minute or two was all the publicity they had actually received. There was a clear intent to deceive, but the celebrity merchant who collected thousands for orchestrating such a ruse had no problem with his offer. Technically our colleague's business did appear online on a site related to the media outlets, but the entire venture reeked of deception and dishonesty.

Let's now consider the case of a letter you receive with a personalized looking post-it note attached. (See picture below.) This is another form of sneaky tactic, but the level of deception, if any, is subject to debate.

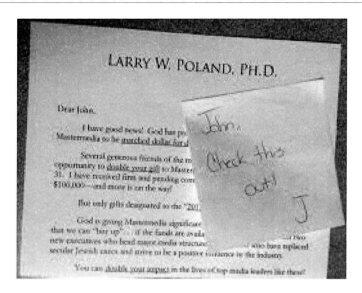

**Personalized Looking Post-It Note on Sales Letter
Designed to Lift Response**

If you are John, the name at the top of the post-it note, you may wonder who "J" is. We have seen unsuspecting (and very gullible) friends wonder for days who could have sent them such a letter. "Who named 'J' would have sent me such a letter?", these people ask themselves for days. They are unaware that the letter falls into the category of junk mail and that it was not sent by someone they really know. It is purely a marketing technique designed to lift response. Marketers have found out that if a person thinks that a piece of junk mail is an authentic letter sent to them by a real person (a form of referral marketing), the recipient is more likely to buy.

Our point here is the extent to which the recipient should know that the letter is junk mail, not a real letter. If you can learn about the sneaky, or some might say ingenious, techniques of marketers by going to the library and doing a little reading, whose fault is it that you had no idea that "J" isn't a real person? Ignorance may be bliss, but here ignorance can lead to an unnecessary purchase.

Some marketers applaud such tactics, whereas others think that they cross the ethical line. (Which reminds us of the following joke – when asked to define "business ethics," Enron executives replied, "What's that?") Here is a case where an actual advertisement from a marketer named Chris Cardell was reported to the Advertising Standards Agency in the UK. Cardell has a very questionable reputation online, with many saying that he doesn't honor his money back guarantee. Others praise his coaching. In any case, the Agency ruled that his advertisement "must not appear again in its present form" and said that it did not meet two of the three advertising standards it was being judged against. So in the Agency's eyes, Cardell's form of marketing was unacceptable. What may be a judgment call or a gray area ended up "going to trial," and one side was the winner. The sneaky form of marketing lost. Part of Cardell's ad and the response from the Advertising Standards Agency is shown below.

lays. My basic message to business owners is – it's not as hard to make money online as you might think."

Over one million people visit Chris Cardell's websites every year o he's clearly practising what he reaches. He also shows business owners such as corporate trainer archie Mundegar how to use powrful internet marketing to attract

Chris certainly walks his talk. Because for a limited time, he's giving away his acclaimed 6-CD set "Essential Profit Strategies" to business owners at www.Profits35.co.uk.

In addition, the first 75 business owners who go to www.Profits35.co.uk will receive, Free of charge, 2-months' membership of his Exclusive VIP Inner

his Six CD Set, 'Essential Profit Strategies' worth £295, FREE and Two Months' Free Membership of his VIP Inner Circle. Go to www.Profits35.co.uk

But please note, you must be a UK business owner to qualify for this exclusive FREE Gift. Go to: www.Profits35.co.uk

truth b
All tion al thing with th ple yo will, b a good your h thing

It looks like a newspaper cutting, but it's an advert for Chris Cardell's membership club. A scam or clever marketing?

The ASA's Judgement Is Very Clear...

"The ad must not appear again in its current form. We told Cardell Media to ensure future marketing communications were designed and presented in such a way that it was clear they were marketing communications, and to ensure they held independent documentary evidence to substantiate claims including those in testimonials, in future."

Chris Cardell, as I understand it, is a former radio ad space salesman turned presenter who switched into selling marketing tips to small businesses. His own marketing efforts appear to know now bounds, seemingly. Sadly this one seems to have backfired.

Here's Somebody Else Who's Been Caught...

This images comes from http://seagalinvestigations.wordpress.com/2010/03/23/clever-marketing-it-certainly-is-not/ - that's another guy who's been "hit" by this dodgy advert.

Partial view of the advertisement ruled unacceptable by the UK Advertising Standards Agency. On the right is the post-it note placed by Cardell on top

To sum up, businesses exist to turn a profit. They will occasionally resort to sneaky and even unscrupulous tactics to gain compliance. Our best advice related to persuasion traces back to the days of Ancient Rome: *Caveat Emptor* or Buyer Beware

VII. Integrating the Four Pillars

We have emphasized that business is about psychology as much as anything else. Marketers who understand what motivates and demotivates prospects will not make the mistake of trying to convince them to buy using levers they don't care about. If your proof is lacking, it doesn't matter how unique your solution is. You need to balance all of the elements that go into persuasion. Business success depends on sales. We began this book with Henry Ford's quote about the importance of sales. Then we examined the four fundamental pillars upon which businesses are built – Message, Market, Merchandise, and Media. In the last chapter, we looked at persuasion techniques, focusing on several key reasons that cause people to behave the way they do.

The Power of Advertising to Build a Business

Let's return to the topic of getting the word out about your business. Every organization, no matter how big or small faces the same challenge of being heard in a very busy and overcrowded marketplace. Perhaps the most undervalued and misunderstood element of business is marketing. And within marketing, an often misunderstood element is advertising. Advertising is one of the key methods of bringing about a sale, and good advertising can literally be the foundation of a billion-dollar company.

As we have already mentioned, we are overwhelmed with clutter. Breaking through the clutter is a major objective for the marketer, and one way to do this is to make your message valuable in and of itself. If your ads are helpful and don't look like ads, they stand a much better chance of being read and remembered. The Cadillac ad that we will review later in this chapter is a great example of this. It looked more like editorial content than the typical ad, and it addressed a subject that is constantly on people's minds.

Anticipating the mind of the buyer is the only real power that the advertiser has, especially when no salesperson is present. We know that the typical buyer "loves to buy but hates to be sold." Another way of putting it is that "people buy for their reasons, not yours." As a result, we need to make our messaging so interesting that it cannot be ignored. Once we know that someone has a problem and we have their attention (the top of the funnel), we can close off their escape routes by offering them a compelling promise backed by hard proof and a solid offer.

Yet even the above is not enough to make someone want to buy now. If the problem is not urgent, there is no need for someone to act quickly. "Do they have a bleeding neck?" is how one marketer puts it. Those who have an urgent pain need a solution fast.

The prospect must also perceive that our solution is one that can't be obtained anywhere else. This is where the Unique Selling Proposition comes into play. If we don't stand out from the crowd, anyone who promises to relieve the pain will do. There is very little to compel the prospect to choose us over the other possibilities.

One way to differentiate oneself is through unquestionable proof. If we are first in the market and have the most market share, this is compelling evidence of our leadership. Or we may have perfected a process that no one else has yet to duplicate. Proof that we are unique and capable can come in many forms and is practically a requirement in today's hyper-competitive world.

The final piece of the puzzle is our offer or proposition. It must be one that resonates with the prospect's buying criteria. If we emphasize a wide selection of colours and they value fast delivery instead, there is a mismatch. We must make our proposition easy to understand and easy to accept. When we combine it with the other elements we have just looked at – a unique, compelling promise and hard, undeniable proof – we have a winning message or advertisement.

What about price? Certainly, there are those who shop for low prices but let's not forget that quality and value are also important. Do you look for the cheapest doctor? No, you look for someone who is competent. When you are able to present benefits and value that fit with what the prospect is looking for, price becomes less of an issue. In addition, your USP can weed out those whose buying criteria don't fit what you offer. If you are positioned at the lower end of the price scale, those seeking to pay more for a higher level of service should recognize that right away. As Bencivenga says, "the more you increase desire with your promise, uniqueness, and proof, the higher price you can charge."

Creating effective advertising is often seen as something of a black art, with "creativity" held in high regard regardless of whether the advertising brings in sales. Measuring the return on this category of marketing investment has long been difficult, especially for advertising that is brand oriented, or, as some put it, "keeping your company's name in front of the customer." Who knows how many people bought a car as a result of watching an ad during a sporting event?

On the other hand, we have direct response advertising. One of the most innovative and important advertising agencies that helped usher in modern marketing is the firm J. Walter Thompson Worldwide, founded in 1864. The style of advertising they advocated, and the type we are focusing on in this book, seeks a response on the part of the reader. Rather than simply promoting a product with flowery language and cute images, such advertising has the intention of moving people to action.

In the early 1900's, Thompson and his colleagues gave a series of talks on advertising and its importance. They are noteworthy for their insights and simplicity. In today's era, when marketing has evolved into multiple disciplines based on the analysis of mountains of data, it is refreshing to come across timeless principles that have universal applicability. Here is an excerpt from the talks:

J. Walter Thompson

Timeless Principles

There are many manufacturers who do not advertise because they do not understand advertising. They know that it means an outlay of money, but the results seem to them too far away, too uncertain and too intangible for conservative business.

If you are wavering in the borderland of doubt and decision, we want you to devote a quarter of an hour to a quiet consideration of these points:

1st. If advertising were not a practical and highly efficient method of building trade, do you suppose hard-headed American merchants and manufacturers would invest several hundred millions of dollars every year in advertising space? Look through any standard magazine or large daily newspaper, and make a note of the names of the advertisers. Then turn to these names in Dun or Bradstreet. Almost all of them have first-class ratings. They are substantial concerns.

2nd. Observe that the great majority of periodicals and newspapers print more advertising than reading matter. They do this year after year. Somebody pays for it, and finds it profitable, or it wouldn't be continued.

3rd. An expenditure of money is required for advertising, but an expenditure is required for anything that is worth doing, from having your windows washed to buying your stock of goods for next season. You need not necessarily begin your advertising with an appropriation so big that you have to mortgage your plant to raise it. Most big and successful advertisers started their publicity with small and careful expenditures. Advertising has the peculiar quality of being adjustable in circumstances. You can spend a thousand dollars a month or a hundred thousand, and make it profitable in either case.

4th. Any businessman can understand the whole advertising situation in an hour. To understand it, you don't have to acquire a technical knowledge of type, cuts, and rates per line. Your advertising agent will attend to the details.

5th. Don't fall into the mistake of believing that the results of advertising are far-off and visionary. On the contrary, it is the most rapid method of selling ever devised. By means of publicity, you can cover the country in a month.

A few comments. You may have noted that "several

hundred millions of dollars" were spent every year on advertising in America. Today, in 2016, that figure is over $200 billion. That's over a 200-fold increase. And, of course, there is a lot of advertising that doesn't cost money. One has to ask why millions of companies would spend vast sums on advertising if it didn't work. The answer is that they wouldn't.

As Thompson observes elsewhere, "You don't have to convince the average American to sell him your goods. You have only to half-convince him, and he does the rest. The vivid imagination of the American public is in the background of every story of successful advertising."

In other words, advertising has to do with combining desire, longing, and imagination in the quest for progress and a better life. If you wrote down the main things people all over the world strive for, there aren't that many: good health, money, happiness, sex, love, intimacy, friends and family, well-being, power, and a few others. Years ago, there was an ad that contained the following line: living well is the best revenge. Living a good life is often a main ambition, no matter whether you were born to luxury or in a poverty-stricken desert country. Human wants and needs are similar, and they always will be.

But let's get back to advertising. Advertising isn't always going to create sales by itself, but it will help get the attention that every business desires. Sometimes the purchase decision is more complicated than simply reading an ad, but the ad can open the door for future consideration.

Another point in the Thompson talk is that "an expenditure of money is required for advertising." Leaving aside free advertising for a moment, one reason that businesses have had such a hard time with advertising is that often they aren't sure what works and what doesn't work. Measuring the effectiveness of advertising has long been difficult and time-consuming. Today, digital marketing gives advertisers the ability to track and measure response almost instantaneously, which is one reason Google has become one of the world's most valuable companies. Instead of just throwing money into the wind with television advertising, billboards, and newspaper inserts that may or may not have an effect, advertisers can now micro-target their audience and determine whether a light blue background was more effective than dark blue. Such precision has changed the game tremendously.

We were struck by the line, advertising "is the most rapid method of selling ever devised." When Thompson wrote these words, the advertising profession was in its infancy. Yet this statement rings just as true then as it did before. If you want to build a business, getting coverage and being seen are critical elements. There are any number of ways to get attention for free, but "pay to play" is one way of assuring that you will be seen. The phrase "paid media" refers to paying to get your message into the market, and in a capitalist society, it has a major role in the dissemination of news and information.

The last point we want to make here has to do with the statement that "you can cover the country in a month." Today, you can cover the country, if not the entire globe, in a minute. Digital advertising can be put into place so quickly that you can start a worldwide business in only a few minutes. Someone in the middle of Idaho or India or Iceland can be seen by more than 2 billion people around the world in the blink of an eye. This presents both opportunities and challenges, as the number one enemy of the advertiser is an overloaded consumer trying to make his or her way through a crowded world. Just because an entrepreneur now has the ability to launch a business practically overnight doesn't mean that success is right around the corner. Billions have been spent on digital ads and digital marketing, and no doubt much of it has been wasted.

The following summary of what makes a good advertising campaign does a great job of removing the padding and fluff that we are so used to seeing. If you learn the principles below, you will be far ahead of many marketing professionals who know all the latest tactics and tips but have no solid grounding in the fundamentals. They think they know what to do, but because they have little knowledge of why to do it, their initiatives are often a misguided effort.

J. Walter Thompson
Key Advertising Guidelines

A plan of publicity, to develop the maximum dollar-efficiency of an advertising appropriation, must rest upon the following conditions:

1st. A useful article at the right price.

2nd. An investment proportionate to the result desired.

3rd. A knowledge of trade conditions and methods.

4th. Study of the article to be advertised, with the idea of determining its selling points.

5th. Selection of the proper advertising media.

6th. Determination of the right time to advertise.

7th. Good copy.

8th. Cooperation with the advertiser in the formation of a complete sales plan, which includes the best means of distribution and the instruction of salesmen.

The function of an advertising agency is to consider these points and work them into an effective campaign.

David Ogilvy, one of the masters of modern marketing, was once asked the definition of good advertising. He said the following:

> YOUR ROLE IS TO SELL, DON'T LET ANYTHING DISTRACT
> YOU FROM THE SOLE PURPOSE OF ADVERTISING.

Ogilvy had little use for brand advertising or advertising that seemed to have no immediate purpose. His ads were put together for one and only one purpose – to sell. This does not mean that a reader is supposed to drop everything and rush off to buy. And certainly, it does not mean only direct response advertising. The classic oyster ad by Ogilvy, shown later, is intended to sell over time, not in an instant. As long as the overall sales purpose of an advertising campaign is not lost, it has a chance of succeeding in causing the desired action, which is to sell the product being advertised.

The rest of this chapter will focus on analyzing several advertisements that have stood the test of time. Some are for brands that were in their infancy a few decades ago. Quaker Oats and Steinway Pianos are leaders in their industries today, but back then they were just ordinary competitors. It was their advertising that helped establish them as market leaders.

All of the ads shown are worth studying carefully for their content, images, layout, and flow. In particular, how does the headline work to draw the reader into the ad? What are the main emotions at work? How will the product or service benefit the reader? If you can answer these questions in the manner that the ad creator intended, then you will be well on your way to being an effective advertiser.

These ads have become classics because they integrated the four pillars and did their intended job. It is important to note that none of these ads follows a formula other than having a headline and body copy. Each is unique and is carefully constructed around the product or service being discussed. Each has a different approach to selling, often the result of extensive research and testing. Many of America's greatest advertisers would spend weeks or even months determining how the four pillars were to work together before coming up with the formula they would employ in their ad campaign. Eugene Schwartz, for example, said he often spent about two months researching and thinking prior to actually constructing his ad or sales letter for a product.

All of the following ads predate the internet and email, with print advertising the predominant medium used. Direct mail letters were also an effective way of getting a message in front of a recipient. The selection of which newspaper, magazine, or envelope to use and whom to mail to is often as involved a decision about the headline and the layout of the body copy.

Ad 1. "They Laughed When I Sat Down at the Piano" – How the Desire to Getting Even Can Launch a Company

John Caples was one of the pioneers of the advertising industry. He wrote many classic ads as well as Tested Advertising Methods, a primer on writing good ads. Many of the headlines Caples wrote have been copied in innumerable ways. For example, "They Laughed When I Sat Down at the

Piano, But When I Started to Play! ~" has spawned imitators selling everything from foreign language courses to tax solutions.

Originally written for a music school, the ad was the inspiration for a website, ViralNova, that in 2015 sold for a reported $100 million. According to BusinessInsider,

> For the last 87 years, scores of imitations used "They laughed when . . . " as a lead-in; sites like ViralNova and UpWorthy are no exceptions. A book of the same name was published in 1959, to teach people the history of advertising, decades before viral content would become a leading player in digital journalism and advertising.

What Caples understood first was that creating the piano ad was not simply about selling piano lessons to those who did not know how to play. Rather, he captured his audience with the promise of emotional benefit; the boy in the ad feels emotion after successfully playing the piano when no one believed in him, and those reading the ad are encouraged to be proud of him and want to replicate that same emotion for themselves ("maybe I can learn how to play the piano, and that can be me!")

The comment about emotions is especially important here. Who hasn't had the desire to show the doubters that they were wrong? Who hasn't vowed to make others "eat crow"? Words have emotional content and are the way into the reader's soul. Words have the ability to take people on a journey and stimulate the imagination like no other form of communication. Putting words together is much harder than it looks, which is one reason good copywriters can command huge fees. One good ad package can move millions in ways that one-to-one communication can't.

A brief aside: In our measurement and the numbers-obsessed world, the word has taken second place. In some circles, the only thing that counts is measurement, tracking, and experiment. Too often what is lacking is a sound foundation underlying what is being measured. We've seen horrible Google AdWords ads that give no reason for someone to click on that ad versus the others that are right beside it. And then the landing pages' viewers are directed to are wholly ineffective at getting the respondent to follow through on the call to action. So in effect, many advertisers track terrible ad campaigns when they should be spending time creating better campaigns, to begin with. And the foundation is the word.

Ad 2. Reading the Mind of the Market: McGraw Hill

Magazines

"I don't know who you are.
I don't know your company.
I don't know your company's product.
I don't know what your company stands for.
I don't know your company's customers.
I don't know your company's record.
I don't know your company's reputation.
Now—what was it you wanted to sell me?"

MORAL: Sales start **before** your salesman calls–with business publication advertising.

McGRAW-HILL MAGAZINES
BUSINESS · PROFESSIONAL · TECHNICAL

The above is a classic by McGraw Hill. We have chosen to examine it for a number of reasons. The copy, set against a stern looking man, reads as follows:

> I don't know who you are.
> I don't know your company.
> I don't have your company's product.
> I don't know what your company stands for.
> I don't know your company's customers.
> I don't know your company's record.
> I don't know your company's reputation.
> Now, what was it you wanted to sell me?

Moral: Sales start before your salesman calls – with business publication advertising.

The ad is selling advertising space in McGraw Hill's business publications, but more importantly, it is teaching marketers what's going on in the minds of prospects. If the person you are calling on doesn't know your company or how your products can help them, they are going to question you. They are going to be confused, which is indicated by the question raised at the end of the list: "Now what was it you wanted to sell me?"

And it is a well-known fact that confused minds don't buy.

McGraw Hill is anticipating what has been given the fancy marketing term called the Customer Frame of Reference (CFOR). You need to see things through the customer's eyes. You need to understand the customer's point of view, which is even more important than your own. Far too many of us put ourselves at the centre of the buying process, which is backwards. (Technology companies are notorious for their attitude that advanced technology will sell itself.)

Another way of putting it for those trying to catch fish is Gary Bencivenga's famous line, "Don't think like a fisherman, think like a fish." If you understand what fish want, and you offer it to them, you have a much better chance of getting a bite or making the sale. Bencivenga claims that fancy lures, expensive rods, and sophisticated equipment are designed to catch fishermen, not fish. If you think like a fish and not like a marketer, you are going to be more successful in catching them.

To generalize, if you as a salesperson or marketer show up at a prospect's door or as a direct mail piece or in their email inbox and they have no idea who you are, what you do, or why you are there, you're going to get a chilly reception. On the other hand, if you've laid the proper groundwork, you are much more likely to at least get a hearing.

Don't get us wrong; you can lay the necessary groundwork even during a cold call or unsolicited email (also known as spam) by demonstrating relevance and competence. If you do so, you have a much better chance of getting past prospect's initial impulse to automatically reject your message before it is even heard. For example, if you give golf lessons, and you say, "Tiger Woods sent me," you're probably going to get a fair hearing. This doesn't mean that the person will buy, but at least they will give you their attention.

What makes the McGraw-Hill ad so important and effective is the psychology behind it. Unless you are supported by an environment that facilitates the buying decision, you are likely to be rejected.

There is an old saying that each of us favors same radio station: WIIFM. The call letters stand for **What's In It For Me**? When we are bombarded with messages, when we are exposed to 3,000 ads a day, the only ones that have a chance of being remembered are ones that answer the question, **What's In It For Me**? You need to speak to the customer's problem, pain, or desire. Notice that relieving boredom or providing escape through books and movies can be a good offer. You don't need to be a doctor looking for a heart attack victim.

The most important ingredient in gaining compliance is furnishing Proof that our solution works as advertised. We can make all the promises in the world, but they are empty until backed up by solid Proof. Testimonials, case studies, success stories, blurbs, and press mentions all contribute to building Proof. You can certainly blow your own horn with promises and claims, but when others do it for you, there is more credibility. Resistance falls, and desire rises.

Ad 3. The Revolutionary Advertorial That Saved Cadillac

Cadillac, c. 1915

One of the most famous headlines of the last century was in a Cadillac advertisement. Cadillac has always been positioned a luxury car. In the early 1900's, Cadillacs cost $2000 or even more, whereas a Ford had a price tag of about $400. In 1915, Cadillac faced a threat from luxury car maker Packard Motors. This company introduced a six-cylinder engine, besting Cadillac's dependable four-cylinder model. In response, Cadillac leapfrogged Packard by bringing out an eight-cylinder, but the car had quality problems. It was prone to fires and short circuits, seriously damaging Cadillac's reputation. Here is the ad. Notice how the headline draws people into the story with the words "Penalty" and "Leadership." The first word, especially, creates a sense of intrigue and mystery, two important keys to advertising and marketing.

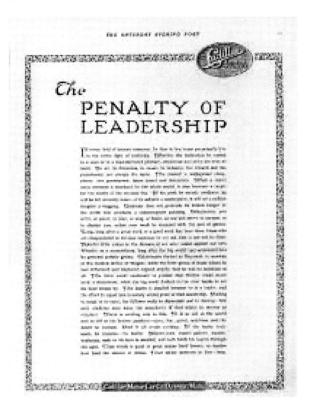

Theodore F. MacManus, who was in charge of Cadillac's advertising program, needed to figure out a way to restore Cadillac's reputation. Its market position as the premiere luxury car maker was in serious jeopardy.

MacManus offered a solution that in retrospect seems ingenious. He himself wrote and placed what we now call an advertorial in the Saturday Evening Post in 1915. It didn't look like traditional advertising; it looked like an editorial copy, hence the description "advertorial." By entering the reader's mind as editorial copy or an article instead of normal paid-for sales and advertising, the message had much higher chance of getting a hearing.

The ad ran only once and was in sharp black and white, compared to a full-colour magazine ad pages so familiar to readers. And nowhere in the copy are Cadillac, cylinders, or even the automotive industry mentioned. The text is about leadership and the pros and cons that go along with it. Other than a small logo in the top right corner of the decorative border and another embedded in the centre at the very bottom of the ad, you would not even know who or what the ad was for.

But the text caused quite a stir and is considered one of the greatest and most influential advertisements of all time. Cadillac's reputation was restored, and Packard Motors has long since gone out of business. On the other hand, Cadillac still stands as a symbol of luxury and high-quality today. In the healthcare field, an upcoming tax on generous health plans was dubbed the "Cadillac Tax" because of what Cadillac stands for.

Note that this is a long copy ad. Many people now and then said that people won't read long copy, but this ad, and many others, proves this theory wrong. Some ads are spellbinding to many a reader, and the Cadillac ad is one example. People requested copies of it, unprecedented for an advertisement. It was as if the text was a talisman. Elvis Presley was so impressed with the message that he supposedly had a framed copy in his home.

Legendary copywriter, Ted Nicholas makes the following observation that we agree with:

"Copy can never be too long, only too boring."

In other words, if your ad is interesting, useful, and engaging, people will read it. The problem is that most advertising is none of the above and is blatantly sales-oriented. Typical ads do not in any way engage or inform, and readers or viewers can spot "advertising" a mile away, causing their defense mechanisms to go up. Advertising that is useful to the reader stands out and gets a hearing.

The sentiments expressed in the Cadillac ad are timeless, which is another quality that makes it stand apart. Leadership is a topic that is forever in demand, as witnessed by the number of books on the topic. On Amazon, there are no fewer than 177,000 books that appear when you search on the word "leadership." We are always looking for the next great leader, whether we are talking about a school principal, a company CEO, or the head of a country.

When asked what made the Cadillac ad work, its creator gave the following opinion: "The real suggestion to convey is that the man manufacturing the product is an honest man and that the product is an honest product, to be preferred above all others." This may well be true, but we think that there is something else going on – casting the market leader in the role of an underdog. The word "Penalty" puts the car maker in the unenviable position of being a target of doubters and naysayers. As they say, "leaders are the ones with arrows in their backs." Anyone who has ever felt the sting of criticism from being a leader rather than a follower can relate.

There are many lessons to be learned from this ad. It is text-heavy and goes against many so-called unbreakable rules, an important fact in and of itself. There is always room for creativity, but to be worth the investment, there must be a business goal in mind. Yet even then, there is no guarantee that any given ad will work. You may have covered every base you can think of, but too many external factors can come into play that will divert attention from your message.

Here is the actual text of the famous Cadillac ad. It still rings true today.

The Penalty of Leadership

"In every field of human endeavor, he that is first must perpetually live in the white light of publicity. Whether the leadership be vested in a man or in a manufactured product, emulation and envy are ever at work. In art, in literature, in music, in industry, the reward and the punishment are always the same. The reward is widespread recognition; the punishment, fierce denial and detraction. When a man's work becomes a standard for the whole world, it also becomes a target for the shafts of the envious few. If his work be mediocre, he will be left severely alone - if he achieves a masterpiece, it will set a million tongues a -wagging. Jealousy does not protrude its forked tongue at the artist who produces a commonplace painting. Whatsoever you write, or paint, or play, or sing, or build, no one will strive to surpass or to slander you unless your work be stamped with the seal of genius. Long, long after a great work or a good work has been done, those who are disappointed or envious, continue to cry out that it cannot be done. Spiteful little voices in the domain of art were raised against our own Whistler as a mountback, long after the big would had acclaimed him its greatest artistic genius. Multitudes flocked to Bayreuth to worship at the musical shrine of Wagner, while the little group of those whom he had dethroned and displaced argued angrily that he was no musician at all. The little world continued to protest that Fulton could never build a steamboat, while the big world flocked to the river banks to see his boat steam by. The leader is assailed because he is a leader, and the effort to equal him is merely added proof of that leadership. Failing to equal or to excel, the follower seeks to depreciate and to destroy - but only confirms once more the superiority of that which he strives to supplant. There is nothing new in this. It is as old as the world and as old as human passions - envy, fear, greed, ambition, and the desire to surpass. And it all avails nothing. If the leader truly leads, he remains - the leader. Master-poet, master-painter, master-workman, each in his turn is assailed, and each holds his laurels through the ages. That which is good or great makes itself known, no matter how loud the clamor of denial. That which deserves to live—lives."

Ad 4. The Longevity of Lysol, a Household Cleaner

Lysol is a household cleaner that has been a staple of households for more than a century. It has been used as a disinfectant, feminine hygiene product, and many other purposes. One reason for its longevity is that during the Spanish Flu Epidemic of 1918, the product was heavily promoted as a way to prevent infection. By using ads as a kind of public service, the product was ingrained into the public's mind as a powerful cleanser. Nearly a century later, the brand is still going strong.

Ad 5. The Ad that Launched Steinway as the Piano of All Pianos

This ad helped vault Steinway to its current position as the piano that tops all others. As any music lover of today knows, few pianos rival Steinway as the one that is perceived as the leading brand. Major concert halls around the world use only Steinways for performances. But this leadership position was built over time. At the time the above ad appeared nearly a hundred years ago, Steinway was only one of many fine pianos on the market.

How did Steinway become the only choice of many performers? Through the process of research that was undertaken to determine Steinway's Unique Selling Proposition.

While researching the market, the ad's creator found that many, if not most, of the leading pianists and composers chose Steinway. This was a revelation that suddenly vaulted Steinway to the top of the heap. The fact that Steinway was held in such high esteem by professionals was an important fact that became the inspiration for the uplifting copy. The Steinway company was reluctant to be associated with the word "immortals" and the artwork in the picture, but market testing showed a very positive response.

The choice of specific and grand-sounding words – "immortals," "supreme piano," pre-eminence," "unquestioned," and "inevitable preference" give this ad a rich and luxurious feeling, much like the piano itself. At a time when piano sales were in decline, Steinway sales began to rise. Today, Steinway is viewed as the piano of choice by serious artists, and this ad shows the power of good advertising. It was instrumental in increasing sales and building a leading global brand.

Ad 6. Guinness Beer Teaches You All About Oysters

The follow award-winning ad by David Ogilvy works for a number of reasons. The first is that it is educational above anything else. If there is any selling going on, it is a soft sell. There is no need to like beer or Guinness to be drawn into the ad. Anyone who enjoys oysters can find something of value, as it is informative and educational. It is helpful rather than intrusive. If you want to know more about oysters, there is something to learn. Even if you don't have a particular liking for oysters, you may be curious and decide to read the copy.

Although it is clear that Guinness is the sponsor of this ad, the brand rides along with oysters and does not overwhelm it. Guinness is trying to create an association between its beer and eating oysters. As we discussed in Chapter 1, making your advertising useful is the core principle at the heart of this ad. It has become iconic and is now available for sale as a poster. Talk about taking advertising to a new level.

Ad 7. Quaker Oats and the Making of a Household Brand

Quaker Oats was at one time just another company trying to succeed in the breakfast food market. They hired Claude Hopkins and said that they would spend a good sum of money, $50,000, to test his ideas. Two Quaker products interested Hopkins, one called Puffed Rice and another called Wheat Berries. Hopkins changed the name of Wheat Berries to Puffed Wheat, and he raised the prices of both products by about 50% so that he had a fair amount of profit for his advertising efforts.

Food Shot from Guns!

Noted scientist explodes a hundred million food cells in every grain of wheat and rice

That's what makes Puffed Grains more easily digested — gives them the nourishment of hot cooked cereals.

Quaker Puffed Wheat *and* Puffed Rice

As he had done many times before, Hopkins performed his initial product research by visiting the Quaker Oats manufacturing plants. He discovered that when puffed, every grain cell exploded, multiplying the grains to eight times their normal size. The phrase "made every atom available as food" came into being as a way to distinguish Puffed Wheat from ordinary cereal. In watching the process where the grains were shot at high velocity to explode them, Claude Hopkins found a unique angle for his advertising that appealed to people's sense of curiosity: "Food shot from guns."

Suddenly, more or less ordinary cereal had a story behind it that was unlike any other. "Noted scientist" adds an aura of authority and credibility that elevate cereal to a scientific discovery. Other advertisers criticized the Hopkins approach, but it was effective in increasing sales by increasing public curiosity. Hopkins also developed a character named Professor A. P. Anderson who was featured in the ads. As a spokesperson, the professor gave life to a company and its products. With the idea that millions of explosions created this cereal, Hopkins elevated the brand and helped create a lasting company.

Although today we may think of oatmeal as the plainest of cereals, at one time Quaker Oats promoted it as brain food that the affluent fed their children. "Where Children Are Fed with Oatmeal" is a famous ad claiming that 7 of 8 affluent households regularly serve oatmeal. The social proof is delivered in the form of an actual canvass or survey. "The Ignorant Do Not" serve oatmeal is another message in the ad. Since no one wants to be thought of as part of this group, the consumption of oatmeal increased. With the urge to give children every advantage so that they can be successful, households of all income levels, especially the middle class, were drawn to the idea that they could achieve higher status by eating oatmeal. Quaker Oats was well on its way to becoming an iconic American brand.

Ad 8. Pepsodent Toothpaste – Changing the Frame from Prevention to Beauty

One of Claude Hopkins' greatest advertising successes was Pepsodent, a toothpaste that is still sold today. Its longevity is another testament to Hopkins' power as a writer and advertising genius. Pepsodent advertising was so successful that he continued working on the account for more than twenty years. As was not unusual, his colleagues initially discouraged Hopkins from taking on the task, partly because Pepsodent was premium priced at double that of the average toothpaste.

Make This Test

See how teeth glisten then

This ten-day test costs nothing. To millions it has brought a new era in teeth cleaning. This is to urge that you try this method. Then let your own teeth show you what it means to you and yours.

To fight the film

The object is to fight the film which causes most tooth troubles. Film is that viscous coat you feel. It clings to teeth, enters crevices and stays. The old methods of brushing do not end it. So

despite all care, tooth troubles have been constantly increasing.
It is the film-coat that discolors, not the teeth. And nearly all teeth brushed in old ways are coated more or less.
Film is the basis of tartar. It holds food substance which ferments and forms acid. It holds the acid in contact with the teeth to cause decay. Millions of germs breed in it. They, with tartar, are the chief cause of pyorrhea. And that disease has become alarming in extent.

A daily combatant

Dental science has now found ways to daily combat this film. For five years the methods have been carefully watched and proved. Now leading dentists everywhere advise them.

These methods are embodied in a dentifrice called Pepsodent. Millions now know it and employ it. Wherever you look the results are seen in glistening teeth today.

Acts in five ways

One ingredient in Pepsodent is pepsin. Another multiplies the starch digestant in the saliva to digest starch deposits that cling. The alkalinity of the saliva is multiplied also. That to neutralize the acids which cause tooth decay.

Two factors directly attack the film. One of them keeps teeth so highly polished that film cannot easily adhere.

With every application, Pepsodent combats the teeth's great enemies in new and efficient ways. To millions it is bringing cleaner, safer, whiter teeth.

Send the coupon for a 10-Day Tube. Note how clean the teeth feel after using. Mark the absence of the viscous film. See how teeth whiten as the film-coat disappears.

This test will be a revelation. Make it now. Cut out the coupon so you won't forget.

Pepsodent
PAT. OFF.
REG. U.S.

The New-Day Dentifrice

A scientific film combatant combined with two other modern requisites. Now advised by leading dentists everywhere and supplied by all druggists in large tubes.

10-Day Tube Free

THE PEPSODENT COMPANY,
Dept. 510, 1104 S. Wabash Ave., Chicago, Ill.:
Mail 10-Day Tube of Pepsodent to

Only one tube to a family

In order to find the angle that he wanted to use in his advertising, Hopkins conducted extensive research on the product and its benefits. After much study, he came upon an obscure note that gave him the foundation for his advertising. He discovered that Pepsodent removed "mucin plaques" on teeth. Hopkins changed the term to "film," and it was this simple observation that became the centre of his campaign. Hopkins started promoting the toothpaste as a way to beauty simply because it removed film from teeth. It didn't matter if other toothpaste did the same – he was the one who made the idea a household fact. He created a 10-day test so that people would see how white their teeth could be. The use of the mirror in the above ad shows people admiring their own teeth, an ingenious way to get readers to identify with the characters. Everyone has looked at himself or herself in the mirror, and what we see in the ad is something of ourselves.

It is important to point out that Hopkins decided that rather than promote toothpaste as a way to prevent film from developing, it would be better to promote it as a way to achieve beauty. People rarely buy prevention but instead, prefer to buy solutions. This is human nature and gives rise to the phrase "an ounce of prevention is worth a pound of cure." As Hopkins wrote in his classic book **Scientific Advertising**, "People will do much to cure a trouble, but people, in general, will do little to prevent it. This has been proved by many disappointments."

For you as a marketer, look for positive benefits and rewards that you can promise instead of misfortune or illness that you can prevent. And see if you can find a reason for people to buy now rather than wait and buy later. As Hopkins said, "People are seeking happiness, safety, beauty, and content. Then show them the way. Picture happy people, not the unfortunate. Tell of what comes from right methods, not what results from the wrong. For instance, no toothpaste manufacturer ever made an impression by picturing dingy teeth. Or by talking decay and pyorrhea. The successes have been made by featuring the attractive sides."

VIII. Conclusion

The 5 Universal Sales Objections

1. No time
2. No interest
3. No perceived difference
4. No belief
5. No decision

Gary Bencivenga

We have now covered the Four Pillars individually and shown how they work together with persuasion techniques to move us to action. Advertising is the purest form of salesmanship, as it potentially speaks to millions at once, attempting to do the heavy lifting of getting someone to comply with a request.

Now it is time to reinforce that they work as an integrated whole and must fit together. Think of the pillars as pieces of a puzzle. If any piece is out of place, the puzzle can't be solved, and the entire effort will suffer.

The Pieces of the Puzzle Must Fit Together

Although you may think of yourself as a shrewd marketer, examine your own advertising. You may find that unproven promises dominate and that proof is thin. Yet people buy on proof. Unless we back up our claims, we will be viewed as those who offer empty promises or even liars.

If you are new to business, you may lack proof even though you have all the credentials in the world. Jay Abraham, who often uses the term "ethical persuasion," offers a reward or bonus for those who give him a testimonial. In that way, he has amassed thousands of detailed testimonials stating how he has helped the author increase sales, profits, accounts, market share, and the list goes on and on. When people see the amazing number of testimonials that all sing his praises, social proof begins to work. *"If so many people say great things about him, he must be good,"* the thinking goes. Abraham is a bonafide top-line consultant, and he has a book of well over 500 pages filled with nothing but testimonials.

The Importance of Innovation and Analysis in Advertising

Despite billions of dollars spent by merchants studying persuasion and marketing in academia and the real world, there is no foolproof method of advertising any given product so that people will buy. There is no way of crafting a message, so that is guaranteed to resonate with its intended audience. Even though human nature does not change, circumstances and tastes change. What could be a great deal today might be a terrible one tomorrow.

Eugene Schwartz, the author of Breakthrough Advertising, said that "No formula works twice. What will work? Innovation, of course." He adds, "In a field in which the rules are constantly changing – where the forces that determine the outcome are constantly shifting – where new problems are constantly being encountered every day – rules, formulas and principles simply will not work. They are too rigid – too tightly bound to the past. They must be replaced by the only known method of dealing with the Constantly New – analysis."

To put it another way, the marketer's job is to analyze the temperature of the target and make sure that the messages, offers, and delivery vehicles are in sync with the target's attitudes and behaviors. You may have the greatest mousetrap in the world, but if no one has any mice, you are doomed.

As we quoted at the beginning of this book, Ecclesiastes said, "there is nothing new under the sun." Obviously, this is not quite accurate, as each day brings new innovations and developments into the world. But the fundamental motivators such as money, health, sex, love, longevity, freedom, and power will never change, only the scenery. As marketers, it is your job to find a way to channel timeless desires and emotions them towards your offering.

Acknowledgements

In the Bible, a very old book if there ever was one, Ecclesiastes says, "there is nothing new under the sun." If that's the case, we're not exactly sure what all of us have been doing for the last 2,000 years. Is there anything called originality? Have all of us been simply repeating what was said eons ago? Regardless of the answers, we make no claim that we are the first people to put forth the ideas in this book.

Someone once said that creativity is the art of concealing your sources, but we don't want to conceal anything. We want to pay homage to many who have gone before us. We have learned from them and incorporated many of their research and teachings into our thinking and approach. People like Jay Abraham, Robert Cialdini, Gary Bencivenga, Claude Hopkins, David Ogilvy, Dan Kennedy, Daniel Kahneman, Wendy Lipton-Dibner, Dan Ariely, Gary Halbert, Joe Sugarman, and many others. If you don't know their work, we encourage you to do a little investigation. The above have made significant advances in getting to the heart of what makes a business successful, and they've got a lot to say. We don't want to play any favorites, but some of their work is absolutely a must-know. If you prefer to try to navigate through the shark-infested world of business without a proven guide, that's up to you.

Joseph Campbell and the man he called his best student, Star Wars creator George Lucas, have also had a profound influence on us. Campbell showed how the Hero's Journey is a central element of the human story, and Lucas has taken that theme and built an empire around it. Many thought the first

Star Wars film was something of a joke and would die a quick death; instead, it was the beginning of an odyssey that shows no signs of slowing down nearly four decades later. Star Wars: The Force Awakens, has surpassed the $1 billion in ticket sales in short order and has cracked the Top 5 Films of all time just a few weeks after its release.

About the Authors

Rick McCulloch is an Author, Speaker, Business Development coach and the C.E.O. of Entrepreneur Solution. He is a master synthesizer who applies the best in business and scientific thinking to client problems. His specialty is helping find their Breakthrough USP in order to skyrocket sales. In addition, he accelerates growth and engineers success by helping others successfully market to the emotional part of the brain where buying decisions are made. He has a Bachelor's degree from the University of Manitoba, a certificate in internet technology from the Southern Institute of Technology, where he has also been an instructor in the sciences, and a certificate from the Dale Carnegie Institute. He is a member of the Canadian Imperial Business Network, a past member of the Junior Chamber of Commerce and the Calgary Chamber of Commerce and a Founding Member of NEURS, a global organization dedicated to helping entrepreneurs succeed. Rick is a self-taught entrepreneur having studied marketing and business masters such Brian Tracy, Jeffery Gitomer, David Allen, Jay Abrahams, Meir Ezra, JT Foxx, Charlie Cook, David Neagle and Perry Marshall. He has directed marketing efforts for US based software companies. He currently also mentors students and new graduates from the geosciences, in career management and volunteers for the Earth Science for Society, in association with the Association of Engineers and Geoscientists of Alberta, of which he is a member. He is connected with many entrepreneurs worldwide as a result of attending international events like Mega Partnering. He recently published "Timeless Commandments for Entrepreneurial Success".

David Shiang is the President of Open Sesame Marketing & Communications, a consulting and coaching firm specializing in helping clients make quantum leaps in their businesses and personal lives. David is a graduate of MIT and has a Master of

Management from the Kellogg School at Northwestern University. He was also a Danforth Fellow in the English Ph.D. program at UC Berkeley. He has broad experience in marketing, strategy, coaching, consulting, research, and education. He began teaching marketing in 1989, designing programs for companies such as GE, Chase, and DuPont. He was VP of Software Consulting with a division of IDG, a $3 billion global technology media, research, and event company. He has worked with entrepreneurial firms as well as companies such as Microsoft, IBM, and HP. He is the author of God Does Not Play Dice: The Fulfillment of Einstein's Quest for Law and Order in Nature and The Regret Cure: How to Eliminate Toxic Emotions and Never Regret Again. He is also the world's leading authority on Jim Morrison and The Doors. He co-hosted Skyrocket Your Success 2013, a 3-day entrepreneurial marketing summit, and has presented at the Billionaire Event with George Ross of the Trump Organization, The Nido Qubein Experience at High Point University, and other key leadership gatherings.

Rick McCulloch may be reached at
rickm@entrepreneursolutionsinc.com

David Shiang may be reached at
dshiang@entrepreneursolutionsinc.com

What Satisfied Clients Say

"Rick made us look real hard at the way we do things and were able to identify the problem we had and fix it within minutes. As we progressed through the Powerpoint, the picture became very clear, and the solution was right there to answer the questions we had for the last couple of months.

In my opinion Rick's course is something that everyone should take and for sure this course would fit well for those starting a new business and no later than a year into the start-up to make sure that the system that the business is using are arranged in proper order, and the people involved will identify the weak areas before they become a problem that could ruin a business. Both sessions have left us with great ideas that we are aggressively pursuing and assisting us in finding a new energy that motivates us moving forward, knowing we are improving and moving in the right direction."

~Jim Linnell, CIBN Member and President, EcoPower Industries Inc.

Rick has been very helpful in "pointing me and my business" in the right direction to accelerate growth within my company. I am extremely grateful for his guidance as well as his expertise in business development.

~Bonnie Armstrong, Mobile Marketing Allies, President

Rick's seasoned mantras are bound to consolidate all your stray thoughts and incoherent wishes into a roadmap for your dreams to come true. His vast years of experience in dealing with complex situations can provide you the ease and comfort in your journey towards a successful entrepreneurship.

~Satyendra Sinha, Entrepreneur

I had the pleasure of meeting Rick through business. Rick is a highly intelligent professional who presents his discussions and explanations based on experience and well-rounded. research.

~Ryu Tokumine, Entrepreneur

Rick is a very honest and sincere Person. He has gone through tremendous efforts on himself to help guide you to where you want to go in life both personally and professionally.

~Wes Anderson, World Financial Group

Rick McCulloch is a dedicated service-oriented delivery individual with a passion for mentoring and impacting knowledge and business development skills in the lives of those he comes across. He is honest, loyal, friendly and pragmatic and is one who goes the extra mile to get a project done even when the reward is not imminent. I found my time networking with Rick very rewarding and will recommend his book any time any day.

~Olubiyi Ishola, MSc, P.Geo.

My team hired IDC to conduct research and deliver a set of white papers for Microsoft's sales force. David was the project manager and the glue that kept the project together.

~Bill Barna, Microsoft Practice Director – Energy

David is an innovative marketer who understands information technology, and he has read more books on marketing and sales than anyone else I know.

~David Alexander, Web software guru

David is one of the most brilliant people I know, and I was privileged to work with him for more than 3 years. He has a firm grasp of what's required from a service provider - he can determine a client need, articulate their requirements and execute a solution.

~Maire Kushner, Principal at CreativeMarktingContent.com

A Special Offer for Qualified Businesses

Entrepreneur Solutions offers a **Strategic Assessment** that will give you and your business more focus, clarity, and control. Here is the goal of this fast-paced, no-nonsense session:

1. Gain more clarity around your goals and what is holding you back from achieving them.

2. Pinpoint the specific roadblocks in your business that you must remove in order to make your path to success easier.

3. Identify ways to accelerate your progress with little-known shortcuts, tips, and techniques that apply to your specific situation.

By the end of the Strategic Assessment, you will have greater insight into your business and the specific actions to take in order to succeed. To find out more about how you can take advantage of this limited opportunity, go here:

Assessment.SkyrocketYourProfit.com

Continue your journey to success

by getting free copy of my book

"Timeless Commandments for Entrepreneurial Success"

At

tcfes.skyrocketyourprofit.com

Breakthrough USP Marketing

Skyrocket Your Sales 20% in 90 Days Without Spending More on Advertising - Guaranteed

Catapult your sales with a powerful Unique Selling Proposition (USP) that makes you stand out from all your competitors. If you don't give your prospects a compelling reason to do business with you, they will go somewhere else. A million dollar USP can take an unknown company and turn them into a famous somebody. It's the difference that can take a product or service from "good" to a marketing "great."

A breakthrough USP is one of the core marketing vehicles through which great financial fortunes are made. Think of FedEx and Domino's Pizza, companies that redefined their industries while becoming billion dollar enterprises. Crafting and communicating a compelling USP is the most important thing you should do before anything else with your marketing. You need to figure out what in the world you stand for and let others know your true passion.

If you can't differentiate yourself, if you can't give a reason why you're unique, then your sales scripting, messaging, advertising, blogs, partnerships, community marketing will be like everyone else's. Craft a powerful USP that hits a home run in the mind of your target market, and you've found the one thing that can bring you out of obscurity into the spotlight of fame. A properly designed and executed USP Is Pure Marketing Gold, and Breakthrough USP

Marketing will help you get it.

Why Breakthrough USP Marketing from Entrepreneur Solutions?

Breakthrough USP Marketing is a 3-month structured program that is guaranteed to produce a 20% increase in sales (if not much more) within 90 days or less. After formulating a powerful USP through research and testing, we make the USP an integral part of the fabric of the business. We leverage the available assets in your business (many of which are hidden from view), including your database of customers, partners, and prospects. We also search for partners and alliances that can broaden your reach without a major investment on your part. With your help, we rethink your business from top to bottom, looking for leverage points in places you may have never thought to look.

Your satisfaction is fully guaranteed. We will work with you until you experience the results promised. And with our Pay As You Go method, your investment in the program will come from increased sales and profits. You won't spend a dime on additional marketing or advertising as with other sales consultants.

Participation in Breakthrough USP Marketing is strictly limited due to its unique performance guarantee. For more information and to find out if you qualify, contact

Rick
rickm@entrepreneursolutionsinc.com
+1.403.910.0311

or David
dshiang@entrepreneursolutionsinc.com
+1.781.856.8142